Puppy Training 2021:

A Step By Step Guide to Positive Puppy Training That Leads to Raising the Perfect, Happy Dog, Without Any of the Harmful Training Methods!

Jenna Jimenez

Table of Contents

Introduction

Congratulations on purchasing *Puppy Training,* and thank you for doing so.

The following chapters will discuss all of the things that you need to know in order to get started with training your new puppy. Bringing home a new addition for the first time can be a really exciting endeavor. The whole family may have spent time picking out the puppy that they wanted to bring home, and now they are excited to bond with her and to make some lasting memories.

But before this happens, you need to make sure that you train the puppy in the proper manner. This is the best way to ensure that the little one is going to be able to avoid having accidents, does not get aggressive, and is able to follow the commands that you give to them. Once this is all in place, your puppy will be a valued member of the family, who also behaves and acts in the manner that you would like.

This guidebook is going to walk you through the steps that you need to follow in order to get your puppy trained and ready to behave. To start, we are going to prepare for the puppy by getting the supplies to make her feel at home. Then we will move on to some of the things to expect when you bring the puppy home the first few days with the puppy, the golden rules of dog training, and some of the basic stages that you need to keep in mind when you start to train a new command to your puppy.

Once we have some of those basics down, it is time for us to move into some of the actual training methods that you are able to use. We will look at crate training your puppy, how to house train your puppy, and some of the reasons that positive reinforcement, rather than negative reinforcement, will be so important when it comes to all of the training that you decide to do with your puppy.

To end this guidebook, we are going to move into some of the fun commands that you can teach her. Even if we miss a few that you want to work with or some of the tricks that can be used with your new puppy, you can still use tips and methods that we discuss to work with those commands as well. We will finish off with some tips on how to deal with any separation anxiety that your puppy may have when you or someone else in the family leaves. We will also discuss how to deal with some of the tough dog problems that can sometimes develop in a new puppy in your home.

Bringing home a new puppy is meant to be a great experience for the whole family. But you can make it even better when you stop and train her on the behaviors that you see as acceptable and the ones that you would rather they learn how to avoid. When you are ready to learn some of the basics that are needed to train your puppy, make sure to check out this guidebook to help you get started.

There are plenty of books on this subject on the market, thanks again for choosing this one! Every effort was made to ensure it is full of as much useful information as possible. Please enjoy!

Chapter 1: Preparing Your Puppy

Getting a new puppy to add to your family can be an exciting thing. Whether you are getting your first dog, and you want to make sure that they can acclimate with others in your home, or you have had a few in the past, and you want to make sure you get it right this time and that there are no issues between the different dogs in your family. No matter the case, this is a time that needs a bit of preparation. There are a few things that you will need to get organized before you bring home the new puppy to ensure that you are prepared and that everything goes as smoothly as possible.

Budgeting for the Puppy

If you are truly ready to bring a puppy into your home and raise them, make sure that you don't overlook the financial part of the process. One of the biggest mistakes that a new dog owner is going to do is to adopt a new dog without properly budgeting for the recurring costs that a dog is going to generate. It is best if you are able to come up with a good budget right from the start, before you even bring the puppy home, to ensure that you are fully aware of how much it will cost and whether you are able to fit this into your life right now.

The Preparation List for Your Puppy

The next thing that we need to take a look at is how to prepare for the puppy. As part of the budgeting process that you are trying to work with, you are going to need a few supplies to make things easier. You should consider purchasing most of these items before your puppy comes to your home. This will make sure that you are set and that the puppy is going to feel right at home with you. Some of the items that are going to be important includes:

1. The dog crate
2. High-quality dog food
3. Food and water bowls
4. Treats that can help you with training
5. Any toys that you would like to use with them.
6. Items to chew on so that they won't have to chew on furniture or shoes.
7. Leash, collars, and harness
8. A baby gate if you want to keep the puppy in one area of the house.
9. A brush for the dog
10. Toothpaste and toothbrush for the puppy
11. Ear cleaning solution
12. Bath supplies like nail clippers and shampoo for the dog
13. Poop bags for when you go on walks.
14. Treat pouch and carrier if you would like to have this.
15. First-aid supplies
16. Tick, flea, and heartworm protection.

Let's take a look at some of the things that you need to have and some of the different reasons that you would want to use these items.

First on the list is the crate. The crate can be important to use because the puppy is going to be a den animal, and they thrive when they have their own space to feel safe and secure. It is important for their well-being to have a safe place where they can go in order to relax. It is also great for the behavior of your puppy and their mind. It allows them to get away from the things that are going to distract them and make them feel nervous and can be a good restart place for them. And the crate helps to make house training your puppy so much easier.

When picking out the crate that you want for your puppy, the size of the dog is going to matter. A small crate is going to make the puppy feel squished, and they won't enjoy it as much. But getting a crate that is too big for the puppy can be hard on them as well. Pick out a size that is perfect for your puppy to feel safe and relaxed in but not large enough to run around in.

The next thing that we need to look at is the dog food. You need to pay special attention to the foods that you provide to your puppy because it will help with the dog's physical and mental development. There are a few different kinds that you are able to choose from here, and they include:

1. Raw feeding: This is going to be a diet that relies on raw foods for your dog and allows the digestive system to eat what is all good for them, rather than the processed foods. This is usually more expensive to work with, but if you are able to do it, you will see some great results.

2. Kibble: This is the method that most people are going to work with because it is easier and less expensive. There are some great kibbles out there, but you do need to double-check the kind that you are using, stay away from any that have added color in it, make sure of all the ingredients that are inside, and stick with kibble that is grain-free. There are plenty of natural and nutritious options to choose from. Do your research and see what you can afford for your pup's health.

Once you have picked out the kibble or food that you want to use, it is time to pick out the right water and food bowls to use for your pet. When it comes to the water and food bowls, it is fine to use any kind that you would like, except for any that are made out of plastic. The reason for this is that your puppy is likely to chew on the plastic, and this leaves you with a lot of destroyed bowls and the possibility that the puppy will have swallowed some of the plastic. Note also that some dog breeds may need a bowl that sits higher off of the ground.

Training treats are going to be your best friend as you work to train your puppy the right way for them to behave. You will need a lot of these in the beginning. It is best to go with softer treats because these are easier to break apart, so you don't go through as many. There are a lot of good treats out there that help with training. Just read up on the ingredients to make sure they are safe and healthy for your puppy.

And you want to make sure that your puppy has some of their own toys. If you don't provide them with these toys, then you are going to deal with the puppy finding their own, and this could be your favorite pair of shoes, your sofa legs, or something else that is valuable to you. Make sure that you pick out toys that are specifically designed for a puppy. There are some kids' toys that may look the same, but the manufacturers of these are not going to assume that their products will be used by a dog, and this could be dangerous depending on the pieces on that toy.

Always monitor your puppy when they are playing with any of their toys. Dogs, especially when they are young puppies, have a common tendency to chew through and destroy their toys. Don't forget that they are teething! They like to rip the toys apart, which can be a normal part of their play, but if you are not watching for things, it is possible that the puppy will ingest a small part, some of the rope, the stuffing, the fabric or another part that they should not. Monitoring the puppy ensures that you are going to be able to catch them if this starts to happen.

Chewing toys are next on the list. These can be separate from the other toys and are meant to help the puppy as they feel the urge to chew on something. It is much better to give them some kind of toy to chew on, rather than letting them use their own imaginations and chewing up the house. There are many objects that are acceptable for your puppy to chew on, and they will help them to fulfill their need for chewing while keeping the gums and teeth of your puppy as healthy as possible. You can pick out the kind of chew toy that you would like your puppy to have, but a few of the options that are available for you include:

1. Antlers: these are amazing chewing toys for a dog. They are hard, they last for a long time, they are all natural, and they will have the minerals and vitamins that your puppy needs.
2. Bully sticks: These may not last as long as the antlers, but they do last a lot longer than some of the other chewing options out there, they are natural, and they are going to be full of vitamins that the teeth of your dogs need.
3. Himalayan dog chews: These are going to be a healthy kind of chewing object that is made out of Yak's milk. They are going to last a bit longer than the bully stick and can be a nice alternative.
4. Bones: It is possible to work with bones, but you need to be careful with them because they are going to be easier for the puppy to break apart and can cause issues with your dog. If you are going to use these, be careful because you don't want to go with ones that are too soft, like cooked bones, and you want ones that are not going to fall apart.

There are other options when it comes to the chewing toys that you are able to give to your dog, but you do need to exercise some caution with these. You want to pick out ones that are natural, ones that are going to be strong enough to last for a long time and ones that maybe have the added vitamins and minerals that are needed to keep the teeth and gums of your puppy as healthy as possible.

Now we need to take a look at the collar, harness, and leash of your puppy. The collar will come first. There are a variety of collars that you are able to purchase, and each of the styles that you see will serve us with different options. Out of the four most common options that you can go with, the ones that are the most recommended are going to be the first two:

1. The simple collar: This is the common collar that is plane, maybe in a single color, that is flat and will connect with a buckle or a clip to your puppy.

2. The martingale collar: This one is a bit different because it is designed so that the puppy is not able to slip from their collar. It is going to gently tighten around the neck when the dog is pulling on the leash, which can be a good bonus when training.

3. The choke collar: This one is generally not recommended. If it is not used in a proper manner, it can be harmful to your dog, especially when they are still a puppy.

4. Prong collars: This one is almost going to pinch the puppy, which is not the best way to teach them how to walk on a leash. They are not going to be effective, and in some cases, it is going to result in them become more aggressive.

Once the collar is picked out, it is time to take a look at the harness. The harness can be a great tool when you are trying to teach your puppy how to walk on the leash in the proper manner. The harness is going to help with the pulling, helping you to slow them down without adding too much pressure to their neck, and allows you to control their whole body as well. There are several types of harnesses that you can choose based on the one you like and what is going to fit your dog.

The leash is next on the list. You need to have a leash to help the dog learn how to walk around the block any time that you want. There are two options, but most dogs are going to work with the standard leash for the most part. These are easier to work with, come in different sizes based on your type of dog, and so much more. You can also work with a retractable leash, but many people find that this kind can go against what they are trying to do when it comes to training the puppy.

A brush is next on the list. No matter how long the coat of your puppy is, the brush is going to make sure that they are well cared for, that the old hair is removed, and that the new hair is able to grow in well. The type of brush that you decide to use on your dog is going to vary based on the texture and the length of the coat of the dog.

The other things that you may want to consider adding into your home to help you prepare more for bringing the puppy home include:

1. Toothpaste and toothbrush for a dog: Dental hygiene is going to be an important part of the process of raising your new puppy. You should star

brushing the teeth of your puppy from the moment that you bring them home, even though they are going to lose those first teeth. It is also best to work with a dog-specific toothpaste and a two-sided toothbrush. Do not feed the dog toothpaste for humans because the fluoride inside can be bad for dogs.

2. Ear cleaning solution: You also need to add in some weekly ear cleaning when you bring home the dog. There are many choices for this at a pet store in your area. Make sure to get some cotton balls and other items to help make this process easier.

3. Dog shampoo: Dog fur is going to be different than human hair, so you should not use soap or any human shampoo on your dog. Dog shampoo is always the best because it has been created with the dog in mind.

4. Nail trimmers: You also need to spend some time trimming the nails of your dog on a regular basis. If you choose to do this on your own, make sure to get some dog nail trimmers to make it easier.

5. Poop bags: Unless you want to keep using a lot of plastic grocery bags and you want to make sure that you always have enough on hand, make sure to urchase some poop bags.

t carrier: This is going to be an optional part of the process, but it is so that you are able to easily grab out the treats any time an rtunity to train your puppy comes up.

id supplies: Think about some of the first aid needs that your dog ve, and then make sure to keep these on hand. There are even a few companies that make first aid kits that are meant for dogs, and you can pick one up and keep it around in case you need them.

8. Tick, flea, and heartworm preventatives: It is very necessary for you to have these preventative treatments. They do cost more, but they are a very simple measure that can be taken in order to make sure that your puppy stays healthy and doesn't get a bad disease. You can get these at many pet stores or talk to your vet to see which ones are the best for you.

As you can see here, there are a lot of different items that you will need to get in order to work with a new puppy. And it is best if you can get it all gathered up and ready to use before you bring the puppy home. Having this all set up and ready can help to reduce some of the stress that you may be feeling when bringing a new puppy home and ensures that you will be set and ready to put your love and attention on the new addition to your family.

Chapter 2: Bringing the Puppy Home

Now that you have had some time to gather up the items that are needed for your puppy, it is time to prepare to bring the puppy home. Having a good idea of what is going to happen during the first few days with her and how you can make the transition a bit easier will make a world of difference. Let's take a look at some of the different things that you need to prepare for when you finally bring the puppy home.

The First Three Days

Remember that when you bring a new puppy home, the life that they once knew and were used to is going to change up completely. Every dog is going to react to this kind of change, but it is important to know some of the different issues that may occur when you first bring the puppy home.

The first issue to be aware of is sleepless nights. Puppies are similar to babies in that they are going to keep you up for the first few nights. They are going to bark and perhaps cry for the first few nights, and sometimes longer until you have been able to fully crate train.

In addition to the sleepless nights, be prepared for the puppy to have accidents. Even if your dog is a bit older when you bring them home, it is possible that they will have an accident, simply because they are in a new place and they are not sure where they should go. Be prepared for this, and don't feel upset when it does happen. The puppy needs to learn the rules that are allowed in your home so that you can all live together peacefully.

Rules for Feeding Your Puppy

In the beginning, you should make sure that the feedings happen in the crate for your puppy. There are a few reasons for this. First, most puppies are going to be motivated by food, and feeding them in the crate is one of the best ways to get them used to that area. Plus, the crate is a great place for the puppy to be able to sit down and digest their food. To avoid any issues with digestion, puppies should get a rest after they eat. Keeping them in the crate helps to make this happen.

You have to be careful about free feeding the puppy. There are some people who like to use this method to ensure their puppy will get as much food as they need. This advice is bad for the health of your puppy and can really affect how well you will be able to train your puppy. There are a few reasons why free-feeding your puppy may not be the best idea for you or for them, and some of the reasons will include:

1. It can make it easier for your puppy to become overweight. Many puppies are like humans, and if you put out a big bowl of food in front of them, they are going to eat it, even if they are not hungry.

2. When you have food available to them all of the time, it makes the crate and food less appealing. This can take away some of the power of the training treats.

3. It is important for you to keep track of how much your puppy is eating at each meal to make sure they meet their nutritional needs.

4. It is going to lead to you having more accidents. When you are not in control over the feeding times, then it is hard to monitor when your puppy needs to go outside. When you are in control of this, you can learn their patterns and get them outside faster.

5. It makes it harder for you to monitor the healthy habits of your puppy for the long term.

Just like monitoring the food that your children eat, you need to make sure that you are monitoring the food that your puppy eats. Some puppies are going to be light eaters or will be pickier than you would like. But just know that they will warm up to the food if you give it time. Some of the steps that you can use are to only leave the food in the crate for about 15 minutes or so, and then take the bowl completely out of the crate at this time, no matter how much the puppy has eaten. And don't offer any food to the puppy until it is mealtime again.

There may be times when you feel a bit bad about taking the food away and not offering it back to your puppy until it is the predetermined meal time again. But you will find that the puppy will not starve themselves to death if they have food in front of them. If they were hungry, they would most definitely eat it when it is in front of them.

Acclimating the Puppy

Finally, being able to bring the new puppy into your home can be a really exciting thing for the whole family to enjoy. However, there is going to be a little bit of stress that comes with bringing the puppy into the home as well. The best thing to consider here is that the puppy is going through a lot of change. While the dog is going to adapt to these changes much faster than most people do, it is still going to take them a few days to get used to being away from their mother and siblings.

Luckily, there are some actions that you can take in order to help your puppy adapt and get ready to take on some of the new environments that they are in.

First, we need to make sure that we are checking out the essentials. Make sure that, before you bring the puppy home, you figure out what they did before you got them. Depending on the time of day you bring the puppy home, you may want to figure out the last time that they were able to eat and when they were able to go potty.

When you get home, and before you even bring the puppy inside, take them to their designated potty area outside. Let them have some time to explore. This is a brand new area for them, and they may want to figure out what is there and take note of their surroundings. Give them about five minutes or so to see if they will go potty.

Once they have had some time to go potty outside, bring the puppy into the house. You probably do not want to introduce them to each room of the home at this point. Your home can seem really big to a new puppy, and it may really scare them in the beginning. It is best to bring them to the puppy corner and let them have some time to become more familiar with the crate.

Even though the puppy is brand new to your home, it is important to start training them on the right kinds of behaviors from the beginning. It may only last for a few minutes, but put the puppy into their new crate with either a chew toy or some food if it is eating time, as soon as possible. If you find that the puppy doesn't seem to be that interested in what you are offering, offer some new toys or treats until they like something enough that they will be willing to interact with it for a few minutes.

The point of doing this process right away is to help the puppy know more about the crate and get more comfortable inside of it. If you do this introduction to the crate properly, the puppy is going to immediately associate the crate and your home in general with positivity, and this is going to set you up for a great start as time goes on.

Recognizing Some of the Stress Signals

Each dog is going to be different and unique. None of them are going to react in the same manner to the same things all of the time, and that is just fine. The trick is to learn the personality that comes with your puppy so that you are able to react to them and give them the love and attention that they need.

With that said, it is also a good thing if you are able to understand the body language that your puppy is sending to you, especially if they are stressed or uncomfortable around you. Your goal, especially in the beginning, is to learn how to recognize when the puppy is stressed and worried so that you can step in and try to make them more comfortable.

So, this brings up the question of how can you tell when the puppy is feeling stressed out? You will find that the puppy is not going to be like a person, and they won't be able to just come up and tell you that they are feeling anxious or stressed out. As the owner, you need to be able to recognize some of the symptoms that show how the puppy is stressed out and worried. Some of the signs that will show you that your puppy is stressed out will include:

1. Stress yawning: This is going to be a bit different than what you are going to see with a tired yawn. It is going to be done in a more intense manner, and it will be done on a repeating basis.
2. Licking of lips: This happens when there is no food around at all.
3. Pinning ears back: The puppy may decide to have their ears lay down and point a bit behind them.

4. Avoidance: This is when the puppy is going to turn their head away, or they will try to move away.

5. Excessive panting: If you notice that the puppy is panting quite a bit without being hot or tired, this is a sign that they feel a bit stressed out.

6. Growling: This is a very easy indicator to look for. If your dog is growling, then this means that there is something that is causing them to feel uncomfortable.

7. Tail in a lower position: The tail is out low or in between the legs. You may see that only the very end of the tail is actually wagging.

8. You see that the dog starts to bite at their own paws. This is going to happen almost out of nowhere, and the reason that it is happening is that the puppy feels a bit uncomfortable in the situation they are in.

If you bring home the puppy and you see that they are exhibiting a few of these behaviors, then this means they are feeling stressed out and uncomfortable about the situation they are in. it may be time to look around and see what is making your puppy feel this way. Does your puppy see another dog? Do they hear a noise that is loud or unusual? Are there a lot of strangers that are approaching them?

It is pretty natural for the puppy to be nervous when you first bring them home. They are in a new place, surrounded by a lot of new faces that they are not going to recognize at all. Giving the puppy some space to explore and look around and being there when they need you will help them to grow more acclimated to the area. However, if you have had your puppy for some time and you notice these signs start to come up, then it is time to see what is causing it and figure out what you can do to make it better.

Always remember not to scold your puppy when they are dealing with these kinds of emotions. You may not like the emotions, and they may be a bit annoying at times, but this doesn't mean that the puppy is doing anything wrong. They are feeling nervous or worried about something, and they aren't sure how to handle the situation. Learning what triggers your puppy and what you can do to desensitize them a bit so it doesn't bother them or removing them from the situation can help. You may also find that with crate training, your puppy can regulate on their own because they know the crate is a safe spot all their own, a place they can go any time that they need a break or that they need a bit of comfort.

Bringing home a brand new puppy can be an exciting experience for the whole family. Maybe you have been planning out bringing home your own puppy for a long time, and now you finally get to do it! Make sure that you are prepared for the first few nights to be a bit hard to get adjusted to, try and learn a bit about the personality of your puppy, and learn how to tell when she is feeling stressed out or uncomfortable. The first few days are a great chance for you and your puppy to bond together, and giving each time to learn about one another can make this so much easier.

Things to Consider About Grooming

Another thing that you need to consider when you bring a puppy home is how you are going to groom them. Some owners decide to do the grooming on their own in order to save some money, but others like to give that job to a professional groomer in order to get the results that you want. Both of these methods are going to be just fine, as long as you make sure that the puppy gets regular grooming to keep them healthy.

One of the biggest and most costly misconceptions that come with raising a puppy is going to come with grooming and the significant investment that it is going to require on the part of the owner. There are two main problem areas that a lot of dog owners are going to fall into when it comes to grooming, and these will include that they are going to ignore doing any grooming on their puppy completely, or they instill fear into the puppy when grooming is done because they have very little knowledge and grooming protocol.

The first group is going to be those who decide to ignore the grooming of their new puppy completely. When a new dog owner brings home a puppy and finishes with some of the training that we will talk about in this guidebook, they may come to the conclusion that they have met all of the basic needs of the puppy and as long as they feed the puppy, it will all be good.

Make sure that as a dog owner, you don't become this kind of person. It is so important to the happiness and the long term health of your puppy to make sure that they are well groomed at all times.

Then there are those who are going to instill some fear into the puppy about the grooming and will make them feel like grooming is the worst thing possible. This is because they don't know what they are doing, or they don't understand what is going to happen with the grooming. They want to make sure that the puppy is going to be happy and behaved during it, but you need to make sure that you follow all of the steps that come with this.

The first thing to consider here is how to make sure that you get the puppy as comfortable as possible before all veterinary and grooming activities. Some of the things that you can do to make this happen to include:

1. From the time that you bring the puppy home, make sure that you touch them on all the body parts so that they get used to it. This can make them feel more comfortable and prevents aggression and fear when they go to get groomed. Touch their head, open their mouth, touch the nose, ears, feet, legs, and more.

2. Doing this is going to help the puppy be more used to all of that touching so that they are more trusting and more friendly to others who groom them and try to take care of them.

Now, there are going to be a lot of different grooming needs that your puppy is likely to have. Whether you decide to bring the puppy to a groomer that you trust, or you decide to do it all on your own, there are a number of grooming activities that should be done on a regular basis. You want to make sure that the puppy gets their ears cleaned, that the fur is brushed, their teeth are brushed, they get a bath, and nail trimming is done as well.

You can do some of these on occasion at home, but many dog owners like to still set up some regular grooming sessions to make sure that the puppy is getting all of the right care and attention that they need. This also helps to make sure that anything the owner may miss in terms of their health or of the grooming will be caught. If you choose to have a groomer help you with some of these items, make sure that you pick out someone who is reputable and who will take good care of your puppy in the process. Scheduling the grooming sessions every few months, or even a few times a year, will help the puppy get more used to this process and will cut out some of the anxiety and other problems that can come with it.

While grooming may be something that a lot of owners are going to overlook and forget to work with, it is so important for the health and the happiness of your puppy. If you feel comfortable with doing this on your own, you can certainly do it to save some money while still taking care of the puppy. If you don't have the time, or you are worried about doing any of this on your own, then finding a high quality professional groomer can make it easier while still ensuring that your puppy will get the care and attention they need and the healthy grooming that will help them as well.

Chapter 3: The Golden Rules of Dog Training

Now that we have adjusted a bit to the idea of what we need to get and how to bring home the puppy and get them more comfortable in their new surroundings, it is time to take a look at some of the rules that you can follow when it is time to train your puppy. You may not start training the puppy the second that you bring them through the door of your home, but the sooner you start training, the better it is for the whole family. That is why we are going to take a look at five rules that every family with a new puppy should follow. These will make your life easier, can help the puppy adapt to their new home, and will ensure that you can get them trained to follow your house rules in no time! Let's take a look at these five rules and how you can make them work for you.

Use Positive Reinforcement for Everything

The idea that comes with positive reinforcement is that you need to send out a lot of rewards to your puppy when they perform the behaviors that you do like and that you want them to repeat. You can pick out the rewards that you would like to do, including treats, toys, affection, or anything else that your puppy tends to respond to and see in a positive manner. This concept is simple to use, but many families spend too much time on negative reinforcement and then wonder why their puppy is not responding.

This one is going to require a lot of attention from you in order to get the results that you want. Any time that you notice the puppy is sitting calmly, focusing on you when you do tricks, or behaving in any other manner that you want them to, take the time to reward them with your chosen method. The bigger deal you are able to make out of it, the more likely it is that your puppy will continue on with this kind of behavior in the future.

The trick here is to make sure that you are not rewarding the negative behavior. If you ignore the puppy when they are sitting quietly and doing what you want, but then jump up and start making a lot of loud noise and being mad when they chew on the couch, guess which behavior the puppy is going to want to repeat? This is not the kind of reinforcement that you want to encourage

Associate the Name of the Puppy with Lots of Positivity

It is always a good idea to say the name of your puppy in a positive way. If you do need to scold the puppy, do not use their name. When the puppy responds to you

saying their name, even if it is as simple as looking in your direction or coming over to you, tell them "YES" and then provide some kind of reward. This is a good thing to get into the habit of because it helps your puppy to learn early on that hearing their name is a positive experience and that they are going to get a reward of some kind when they hear it.

You may think that this is a silly thing to work with, but when you establish with the puppy that calling their name is a positive thing, then you have taken the first major step needed in order to establish some recall habits that are strong. Then, later on, when the dog is off the leash, and you see that they are about to run off to another dog or go away from you, you will be able to get them to come back and stay with you by saying something as simple as "Rover, come!"

The opposite is going to be true if you try to say the name of your puppy in a scolding tone. If you have done this for a long time, then any time you try to use it in the future, even when doing some training, the puppy is going to wonder if they are going to get a reward or going to get in trouble. They may decide that it is not worth the chance of getting the reward, and they will run off and not listen to you.

Don't Get in the Habit of Repeating the Commands

Any time that you are giving a command to your dog, make sure that you are just saying the command one time. When this is enforced in the proper manner, it teaches the puppy that they need to perform that command right away after only hearing it once. You don't want to start out the training by having to tell your puppy to "sit' a bunch of times before they actually listen.

Now, this is where the positive reinforcement needs to come into play again as well. But if there are times when the puppy doesn't go through and perform the command right after you are done giving it, especially in the beginning when they are learning the process, there are a few steps that you can take to make this easier, including:

1. Try to reinforce the hand gesture that you want to associate back with that particular command.

2. Say the dog's name, a kissy sound, or some kind of sound that will get the focus of the puppy back to you and the hand gesture that you are using here.

3. Learn how to be patient. You do not want to repeat the command, but the puppy Will perform the wanted command if you have patients and get them to focus on you again.

4. When the dog does go through and perform the command or action that you want, be sure to tell them "Yes" right away and provide the reward that you want.

5. Always follow through with what you are asking your dog to do, and remember lots of consistency, and you will be set.

Remember here that if your puppy is not listening or they are too distracted when you give the command, and you have gone through the steps that we have listed above, do whatever it takes to get the puppy to listen to you. You could try to do something that the puppy will find more fun and motivating, lure them over to you with the help of a treat, put them on a leash, or use another option that works the best. No matter what you do here, remember that you do not give this up. This helps the puppy to learn that they need to listen to your commands each time, with no exceptions along the way.

Try the Power of Redirection

Whenever you find that your puppy is doing something that they should not, such as chewing on an object that they shouldn't, you need to tell them "NO" and then find a way to redirect the puppy over to an activity that they are allowed to use. So, if the puppy is chewing on an item that you don't want them to, say "no" and then move them over to one of their chew toys or something else that you will let them have.

Any time that you see the puppy exhibiting a type of behavior that is annoying or that you won't allow, redirecting them over to something else is one of the best ways to make sure they learn what is and what isn't the appropriate behavior in your home.

Too many owners get into the habit of just telling their puppy no, and then they don't add in the redirection to the mix. This is just going to cause the puppy to feel really confused, and they are not going to really stop performing the behavior that they were told to avoid in the first place. This redirection is going to give your puppy the motivation that they need in order to stop doing the behavior.

Training Needs to Always Be Fun

Yes, training your puppy to behave in the manner that you would like is going to be tough. But you also need to make sure that there is an element of fun found inside the training as well. If you are not having a good time, and your puppy is not having a good time, the problems are going to start showing up, and it becomes a lot harder for you to get the results that you would like.

It is best if you are able to make the training of your puppy as fun and happy as possible. This helps the puppy to get excited about the experience, and this is the motivation that they need to listen to you and do what you want. Also, when planning out the training sessions, remember that your puppy is going to have a short attention span, so do not get frustrated when you have done this for some time and the puppy stops listening. Keep the training sessions short and sweet, and fun and your puppy will catch on to what you would like them to in no time at all.

Learning how to train your puppy to do what you want may sound like a lot of hard work. You may be worried that you are going to do it the wrong way or that your puppy will not respond to what you are telling them or doing along the way. But with these five golden rules in place and some of the other tips that we are going to discuss in this guidebook, you will find that training your puppy won't just be a necessity. It will be something fun that you and the puppy enjoy doing together and will help your puppy become a valued and behaving member of your family.

Chapter 4: The Stages of Training a New Command to Your Puppy

At this point, you may have a great plan in place to start training your puppy. You know some of the rules that you need to follow to ensure that your puppy is going to start listening to you and that you both have a fun time when you get going. But at some point, you will want to learn how to teach a new command to your puppy.

Over the time that you have your puppy in your home, it is likely that you are going to want to teach your puppy a lot of different commands, and you want to make sure that it is as easy as possible to work with. That is why this chapter is going to take a look at the top five stages that you need to follow in order to ensure that you can properly train your puppy in any new command that you would like.

Stage 1

The first stage that you need to use when it is time to train a new command to your puppy is to show a hand gesture to lure the puppy and then reward them with a treat and a clicker word. During the beginning of your training, remember that your dog is still learning, and they are working to understand and follow some of the commands that you want to teach them. The basics of the process that you want to work with during this stage include:

1. Give the hand gesture that is meant to go with the command that you would like to teach.

2. Say the command verbally.

3. Lure the dog in some manner to the position that you would like to command them to go.

4. When the puppy listens, it is time to reward the puppy using the clicker word and the treat. Make sure that you do this each time that the puppy performs the command in the proper manner.

Stage 2

Now we are on to the second stage. This one is where you are going to show the puppy the hand gesture, and then when they respond, you will reward the puppy with the treat and the chosen clicker word. Over time, the puppy is going to start making the connection between the hand gesture and the verbal command and his body position. When this happens, it is time to cut out some of the luring that you need to do.

This part is going to take a bit of patience from you. You need to try it a few times and be ready for the puppy to make some mistakes along the way. Your goal here is to give the hand gesture along with the verbal command and then give the puppy a few seconds to see if they will respond to it without the luring. As with all parts of the training, as you move through all of these steps, you are going to be surprised at what the puppy is able to accomplish with a few tries and some patience from you in the process.

Stage 3

Now it is time to move on to the third stage of the training process. In this one, we are going to show the gesture, and then we will reward with the treat and the clicker word every other time. You do not want to go for ten years, having to give the puppy a treat each time they listen to a command that you give. You want them to be able to listen to the commands that you give without having to give them any treats in the long run. This is where we are going to start doing this process.

Once the puppy is able to do the command right away, each time that you command them (both verbally and with the hand gesture), you will want to reward them with the clicker word, but slowly you are going to take the necessary steps to wean the puppy from the treats. This means that you will stick with the clicker word, but you will cut out the treats a bit. Start just giving the treats out every other command.

One mistake that a beginner needs to be careful about is going too fast with weaning off the treats. If you are still uncertain about whether the puppy is ready for this step or not, it is best to go with the treats as a reward for each time you do the command, at least for now. It is so much better for you to reward with treats for a longer period of time rather than nixing the treats too quickly.

Stage 4

The fourth stage of the puppy training process is to show the hand gesture and reward with the clicker word while tricking with treats. This is an important step that you need to get to at some point because it ensures that the dog is going to learn that they need to listen to what you are saying, rather than them just listening to get the treat. No matter if you are holding the treat up so that the puppy can see it or not, you want to make sure that the puppy learns how to be motivated by pleasing you.

So, how are we going to make sure that this will happen? Basically, to make it happen, you are going to present the treat as usual, and then, once the puppy does the command, you will reward them with the clicker word and praise. You can also do this the other way as well. This means that you would have the puppy do the command just by holding up the chosen hand gesture. Once they execute the command, the treat is going to come out of nowhere (your pocket, but it will seem like a surprise).

This is an important thing to try out because it will keep the puppy guessing about whether they will get a treat for doing the command or not. And by default, if this is done at the right time, it is going to help the puppy transition from being motivational with getting a treat all of the time to being motivated without any kind of treat in their face. This is the ultimate goal that you want to reach in order to really see the puppy listen to you, even without a treat present to entice them.

Stage 5

Now we are on to the final stage. With this one, we are going to show a hand gesture, and then we will reward the puppy for listening to the command with a clicker word and a treat on occasion. Once you have been able to get the puppy to consistently listen to the commands that you are giving, you have actually been able to master the hardest part that comes with the training. From this point on, you will want to always work with the clicker word each time that the puppy completes the command that you want, but the treats should be used sparingly by this point.

The point here is that you do not want to have to provide the puppy with a reward in the form of a treat each time that they listen to you. This is going to get more tedious overall and makes it so that the puppy is only listening to you because there is a treat involved. You need to slowly wean away from the treats so that the puppy is going to respond to what you want them to do, regardless of whether they get a treat or not.

You can add in a special treat on occasion, but you should get to the point where you will be able to get the puppy to listen to any command that you say. If you follow the five stages from above, you will be able to make this happen with your training sessions with the puppy.

A Note About the Clicker Word

We spent a bit of time in the last section talking about a clicker word. You have probably seen people who are at the pet store training classes that use a clicker to help them train their puppy. If you are not sure what this is all about, a clicker is going to be a little device that will make a clicking noise any time that you push down on the button. When you are training the dog, the goal here is to make the clicking noise any time that the puppy gives the right behavior, and then pair it up with a treat.

Now, this method may work, but then you have to make sure that you have the clicker on you all of the time. Other people like to use a clicking sound with their voice instead. Your voice is going to be with you all of the time, and this makes the process a bit easier. But you can choose whether you want to keep this clicker around with you, or you want to use a clicking sound with your voice for this training method.

Another thing to consider here is whether you are able to use a good boy or good girl for the clicker word that you use. You can choose to use this, but for the most part, you will want to stick with words that are one syllable long. And you want to make sure that it is some word that you won't say all of the time. If you are able to do this, it is a lot easier to add the clicker or the clicker word, along with the treat, to the end of a command to make sure that your puppy is going to do what you would like them to.

Training your puppy is a process that you and the puppy need to work on together. It is not going to happen overnight. But if you are willing to work through it with your puppy, and you use the five stages and a good clicker word, or even a clicker, as we talked about above, you will be able to really see some results in no time with how well your puppy is going to behave and listen to the commands that you give.

Chapter 5: How to Crate Train Your Puppy

One of the biggest mistakes that you are able to make when you are doing some of the training your puppy is to not crate train them. It is going to seem like a lot of work, but it is going to make your life, and the life of your puppy, so much butter. It does take some patience for you in the beginning, but once it is all done, you will love how easy it is to work with your puppy and provide them with the love and attention that they need.

Some people feel that crate training is going to be a bad thing for their puppy. They feel that it may be a punishment or even inhuman and cruel. But this is not true. In fact, crate training is going to provide the puppy with a safe spot, someplace they can go when it seems like things are getting too much for them. By crate training your puppy, you are basically giving them a safe place that their ancestors have evolved over the years to depend on. Anybody who is telling you that crate training is wrong simply doesn't understand the benefits that this method is going to provide, not just to you but also to your new puppy.

However, one thing to remember here is that your puppy, even though it is good for them, is probably not going to be that fond of their crate at first. They may whine, howl, yell, bark, and more, especially when it is near to the time for bed. And this can end up being frustrating. You have to hold strong here because if you give in, the puppy is going to continue this behavior and won't do the crate training for you.

The number one rule that you have to follow when you are doing crate training is to not allow the puppy out when they are making noise. You do not want to let them out for any kind of noise or sound, whether it is howling, barking, or whining. You may think that letting them out is one of the best ways to get the puppy to be quiet and settle down. But this just makes it harder for you to do the training because it basically rewards the puppy for this bad behavior.

Think of it this way. If the puppy doesn't like the crate and whines and barks a bit to get let out, then you let them out. What do you think is going to be the behavior that they will continue doing? Letting them out because of the noise just enforces the behavior that they were just doing, and if they don't like the crate and they want to get out, they will continue on with the behavior. But, if you make them quiet down before you let them out of the crate, they are going to learn the opposite. They will see that being quiet and settling down is the best way to get out of the crate, and then you can let them out when you are ready.

Your dog is going to respond to the crate in their own unique manner, based on their own disposition and if they have had any experience with a crate in the past. The person who was previously in charge of your puppy may have already had a chance to start with crate training, especially if the dog is a bit older. But if you have a brand new puppy that you just brought home, then this may be the first time they have ever seen the crate.

Now, there are times when the puppy may have been exposed to the crate in the past, but it was not in a positive manner. If this has happened, then you are going to have to approach the crate training in a slow and cautious manner. You may have to take things a bit more slowly compared to other dogs to make sure that they see this as a safe spot to be in.

The best thing that you can do when you work on some crate training is to make sure that you associate as much positivity with the crate as possible. This crate is meant to be a safe spot for the puppy. It is their place to go to rest or when they need a break or to get away from things that scare them. You do not want to start using this as a form of punishment.

Yes, sometimes it is tempting to use this as a way to get the dog to behave or as a form of punishment when you feel mad that they chewed up your furniture.

However, doing this is going to ruin all of the efforts you have made to make the crate a safe spot. The negativity is going to cause the puppy to only see the crate as a form of punishment, and they will not want to go into it any longer. So, the thing to remember here is to only use the crate in a positive manner.

The next thing that we need to explore here is how you plan to get the puppy into the crate and start to use it. Even if your puppy is not that averse to the crate in the first place, you will find that they probably won't run into the crate the first time that they see it. Because of this, you will need to go through and convince the puppy that the crate is just fine to be in and that it can act as their own little den.

The good news is that you are able to use food as a positive tool here. Since almost all dogs are going to be food motivated, dog food is going to be a positive tool that you can use to your advantage in order to get the puppy to the crate. Feedings, in the beginning, need to take place inside the crate. Many puppies will see the food in the crate and will run straight there to get the food. And before long, when the puppy is hungry, they are going to run over to the crate and wait to get their food over there. If you are consistent with feeding the puppy in the crate, they are going to quickly catch on to this kind of behavior.

Of course, it is possible for you to use some other items to associate some positivity to the crate. This can include some of the chewing objects or some toys that are popular with your puppy. Treats can also be another positive thing that you will hand to your puppy if they go into the crate. You do not want to leave the toy or the chewing item alone in the crate with the puppy unattended because this runs the risk of the puppy ripping the toy open and ingesting something that they should not.

The next question that you may have when it comes to crate training is how much time you should leave the puppy inside the crate. While there isn't really a concrete number of hours that you should use the crate, but you should have the entire day of the puppy revolve around the crate, rather than having the day of the puppy revolve around being out of the crate and being free to roam around the house.

This is going to make training the puppy so much harder to do overall. When the puppy can move around wherever they want, this makes it more likely that they are going to have accidents, will destruct many of your personal items (or any that they are able to get ahold of), and you will have a big headache from trying to figure out where your puppy is and where they may decide to go next.

When you decide to allow your puppy to have free reign of the home, they are going to take full advantage of this. This is why creating a structure and setting boundaries for your puppy right from the beginning, so they learn right from wrong, is so important. It is easy to let things slide when the dog is still a cute little puppy, but the sooner that your dog learns the rules and adheres to the principles in your home, the sooner they will be able to gain the freedom to roam around your home later on, without you having to worry about the kind of trouble they will have.

After you have been able to use the crate training for some time, and you are sure that your puppy understands what behavior they are allowed to do, you can then begin the transition of your dog, leaving the crate and gaining more freedom. This process will take some time, and the length of time that it takes is going to depend on the dog and their disposition as well. Some dogs may do just fine if you start to give them some more freedom, and others are going to start misbehaving after you give them some of the freedom. If your dog stops listening and starts causing problems when you make this transition, then it is time to get them back in the crate and work with the structure for a longer period of time.

Wherever the dog happens to be with their training for the crate, it is important that you never use the crate as a way to punish the puppy when they do misbehave. It may be tempting to do this at times, but it is going to disrupt the process of training, and it can really make all of the hard work that you have been doing go to waste.

The whole purpose of working with the crate is to provide your puppy with an environment that is calming and secure for them, a place where they are going to feel safe. But first, you have to make sure that they feel comfortable inside the crate and that they don't feel like it is a punishment. Most puppies want to be able to move around and have freedom, and so they won't be happy to go into the crate. Taking the time to turn the crate into a positive thing, and ensuring that they learn how to use this crate for their own personal space, is going to make life easier.

You may have to take this in stages. It is not a good idea to bring the puppy home, have them just a few days, and then leave them for 8 or more hours in the crate without any exposure. This is going to seem like a punishment since the puppy is not used to the whole process. Crate training is something that takes some time because you have to slowly teach the puppy to get comfortable.

You may start out with five to ten minutes in the crate. You leave the puppy in there for that time, and at the end, you get the puppy to quiet down before letting them out. As soon as you let the puppy out, allow them to have a treat and lots of praise and playtime. This is a good thing to include in your process because it shows the puppy that they are supposed to go into the crate and behave. Just make sure that you don't let the puppy out when they are whining or barking or misbehaving, or this is the behavior that you will become used to seeing when the puppy is in the crate.

Then you will slowly expand the time that they are in there from ten minutes to half an hour, then to an hour, then to a few hours and so on until the puppy is able to stay in the crate for the whole amount of time that you want them to be there. Each time that you come back and let them out after they quiet down give them a treat of some kind and lots of praise. And if the puppy has to stay in the crate for a longer period of time (say that you built them up to a full day of eight hours), make sure that you let them out to the bathroom and take them out to play and run off some steam since they have been so good.

The most important thing to remember here is to not give in to the whining or the howling, or the barking. Your puppy is not going to like the crate in the beginning, and they want to be able to get out of the crate and explore. This can cause a mess. If you give in to the whining and the other issues, then this teaches the puppy that this is the right way to behave, and they won't do what you want in the future. If the whining and howling and barking are too much for you to handle at this time, just walk outside and wait until the time is up.

There are a lot of advantages to using crate training. It can be hard. You don't want to seem like you are mean to the puppy by having them stay in the crate all of the time, especially when they are young, and you are just forming your bond. Remember, this is not causing them any harm, and they just need to have a bit of time to adapt to this new routine.

Once the puppy sees that this is a positive place to be, where they can find comfort, and they get food and fun toys, they will start to go there all on their own. They will start to find that this is the place where they want to be, even when they are given more freedom. And this is also a good step to take to help with many of the training things we will talk about, especially with potty training, because you will find that once the puppy establishes the crate as their den, they will be less likely to want to mess it up or make it dirty. Leaving them there during the day with this idea can help to train the puppy to listen and go outside rather than in the house.

Sample Schedule of Doing Crate Training

We spent a bit of time talking about some of the benefits of working with crate training with a new puppy and some of the steps that you can take in order to make sure that the puppy starts to love their crate and sees it as a positive thing rather than as a punishment or something that is negative. As we also mentioned, it is best if you are able to make sure that the puppy, at least in the beginning of their training, like the crate and has their day revolve around this crate. But how are we supposed to make this happen? Some of the steps that you can take, or a sample of the schedule that you can use, in order to help you get the day of the puppy to revolve around the crate is going to be as follows:

1. Puppy wakes up in the morning already in the crate and then is sent outside to go potty.

2. After this time, the puppy goes back into its crate to enjoy some breakfast. You should let them stay in there for half an hour to an hour to allow the food to digest before they run around.

3. After this time, the puppy will be taken outside to go potty again.

4. Since you have taken the puppy out to go potty, you shouldn't have an issue with having an accident inside. This means that you are able to allow the puppy a bit of freedom here. You can have some supervised playing where you play with them, or you let them wander around and play with some toys, but you are right there.

   a. Since the puppy is out of the crate and hasn't been house trained yet, you can take them out every twenty minutes or so while they are out of the crate to ensure they don't have an accident.

5. After an hour or so of playing, the puppy can be put back in the crate. Leave a chewing object with them for a few hours.

6. Before you feed the puppy lunch, take them back outside to go potty for a bit.

7. Feed the puppy some lunch and let them rest in there to help with the digestion for the next twenty to thirty minutes.

8. When lunch is done and has some time to digest their food, take them outside to go potty again.

9. Allow the puppy to have some more time to play, but keep them under your supervision for this time.

10. When it is time, add your puppy back into the crate. They are likely to want to take a nap during this time, but you can also leave a chew toy in there for them in case this is what they would rather do.

11. After nap time, the puppy needs to go outside to go potty again. If there is time, you can let them have a bit of time to play.

12. It is time for dinner now. This again should last for about twenty to thirty minutes, depending on how long your puppy needs to digest their food and rest.

13. After the food has time to digest their dinner, take them back outside to go potty.

14. Now it is time to let the puppy play for a bit. Keep them under your supervision to make sure that they don't get hurt in the process or cause problems. This is a great time to practice some tricks if you want to do this, or just for the family to play with and explore with your puppy.

15. Before you get ready for bed, take the puppy back outside.

16. Tuck the puppy back into their crate for bedtime. You may also need to take the puppy outside a few times at night to go potty, but this depends on how old the puppy is at the time of the crate training.

Chapter 6: On to House Training Your Puppy

Now that we have had some time to look at the benefits of crate training your puppy and some of the steps that you need to take to make this happen, it is time to take a look at the basics of house training your puppy. For many new dog owners, house training is going to be seen as one of the hardest parts of raising a puppy. However, if you are consistent and do it in the right manner, you will find that a lot of the time commitment and the frustration will be gone. And this is where we are going to start ourselves off with this chapter.

Before we dive in, though, remember that your puppy is going to be an individual, and they will respond to the training at their own pace. There are tips and tricks that you can use that will make the practice a bit easier, but for the most part, each dog is going to respond at their own pace. Don't be persuaded by the marketing pitches of training programs that say how your puppy has to be trained in six days or less. Sure, there are some puppies that can learn quickly, but most will take a bit more time.

What we mean here is that you should not come to this step with a timeline or expectations that are unrealistic. Understanding that your puppy is going to be unique in the manner that they can respond to the training is going to put you at ease and will give you the right mindset to actually get through the house training without a lot of frustration along the way.

The first question that a lot of people have when it comes to house training their puppy is when they should get started. The best option here is to be prepared to begin some kind of house training the moment that you bring the puppy home. Follow these guidelines in order to train your puppy in the fastest way possible and minimize the number of accidents your puppy has in your home.

The first step that you take is to show your puppy the area that is designated for the potty, and this is where you will need to place the puppy each time that you take them outside. The puppy will obviously not go potty in the exact spot each time, but taking them over to this spot when you bring them outside will make a difference. Eventually, the puppy will catch on that this is the spot they need to use to go potty if you do it enough times.

The amount of time that your puppy is going to be able to wait before they have to go outside and go potty will vary based on their age. If you have just brought home an eight week old puppy, then being consistent and taking them out to go potty on a regular basis is going to be the best bet. This is going to be the way that you teach them where and when to go potty faster than before. In fact, one of the best ways that you do this is to take them out to go potty every twenty minutes when they are not in their crate.

Now, there may be times when you bring home a puppy that has been with their past caregiver for some time. It is easy to assume that you don't need to take the puppy outside as often when they are older, especially when they were doing well with their previous home. Of course, you need to remember that when the dog comes home with you, they are in a brand new environment, and they are pretty much starting things over. You may not want to go every twenty minutes when the puppy is older and house trained, but do not go over an hour when they are outside of the crate until they adjust to the new place.

This may seem like a lot of times to take the puppy out, but the more that you do it, the quicker they are going to learn about this process, and the quicker they are going to get house trained. The shorter the amount of time between the breaks to go potty, the faster the house training will go. This results in a puppy that learns the rules of the home faster and will help you to have fewer accidents.

Another tip that you may want to work with while training your puppy is to always bring some treats outside during the potty break. This way, when the puppy does go potty outside, especially when they do it in the designated area like you show them, they can get praise and a reward all at the same time, reinforcing what you are trying to teach them.

The next question that a lot of people are going to have when they work on house training their puppy is what they should be doing when they take the puppy outside. Remember that the routine that you set up is going to be the most effective method to use to reduce the time it takes to train the puppy. When you establish a consistent routine that is associated back with an activity, it is going to start ingraining itself as a habit in the cognitive processes of the brain.

The routine does not have to be super complicated in order to work for your needs. A good routine that can help you to speed up the house training process between you and your puppy could include something like the following:

1. When it is time, you can take your puppy outside to the designated area for going potty.
2. Tell them the command of "go potty."
3. Once the puppy does go potty, give them a treat to let them know that they did something good when they were able to go potty outside. Make sure to give the puppy treats or some physical affection and a lot of praise when they do decide to go potty outside.

It can be as simple as that. In addition to following the steps above for house training, crate training can go hand in hand with house training, and they can work to make the process work better for both of them. One of the keys, in fact, of this is that each time you take the puppy out from the crate, take them right outside to go to the bathroom. If they end up having some accidents in the time they walk from the crate to the door; then you may need to carry the puppy outside so that you don't end up with this kind of issue.

Now, you need to make sure that you are not letting the puppy stay in the crate too long when you are potty training. Most puppies are going to have an instinct to keep their area or their den clean. This isn't going to happen around the house because they can just go and walk away from it. But when you keep them in the crate, they do not want to dirty up the area around them. You can use this to your advantage to work on potty training because the puppy is going to be less likely to have any accidents in the crate.

The problem is that you could be tempted to leave the puppy inside the crate for too long. The puppy has a small bladder, and they are not going to be able to hold it in for 8 hours or more at a time. If you do end up needing to leave the puppy in for longer, then you need to make sure that you or someone else stops by and lets them out once or twice during the day. This helps the puppy to get some relief and will reinforce what you are trying to do with your house training.

You may also run into the issue of the puppy taking a long time to go potty when you take them outside. The first thing to remember here is that you need to be patient. Sometimes the puppy gets distracted and wants to look around and explore the world around them. This causes them to not go potty the second that you take them out, even if they have been stuck in the crate for a long time period before this.

You may find that you need to wait for about 15 minutes or so. The more time that you give the puppy to go potty in the beginning, the faster they will go potty once outside, and the faster you can get the house training done. This may seem like it is going to take forever, and you may be impatient, but just think of how much faster it will make the whole house training process. In the beginning, these 15 minutes may need to be expanded out to 30 minutes or more for the best results.

If you take the puppy outside and wait 15 to 20 minutes and they don't go potty, bring them back inside. Put them back into the crate for a bit, maybe ten to fifteen minutes, and then take them back outside. Repeat this until the puppy does go potty outside, and then give them a big treat and a lot of praise for doing a good job.

This can be hard, and it is going to take a lot of your time in order to see the results. But this is the best way for you to get the house training done. It is also crucial that you actually make your way outside with the puppy and watch them go potty. This allows you to tell if you are actually getting the puppy to go when they are outside. Over time, the puppy will get the process down, and you will be able to give them the freedom to go back outside and inside any time that you would like.

Of course, if you have a young puppy, there are times when an accident is going to happen inside during playtime or the few times that you keep the puppy out of the crate. As the owner, you need to watch how you react to the accident that the puppy is having. This is going to make a difference in how successfully the house training process is going to be. If you catch your puppy going potty in the house (and if you have a young puppy, it is going to happen), then you can do the following steps;

1. Run over to the puppy as quickly as possible.
2. Say "No" in a firm voice to the puppy and then pick up the puppy.
3. Bring the puppy outside right away and bring them out to the area you designated as the potty. Give the command "go potty" to them out there.

It is important that you move quickly during this time. Running is the best. Whenever a puppy is about to go potty in the house, you should sprint over to them and try to catch them before they even start. Even if the puppy is already going potty, get to them as quickly as possible and still pick them up. The puppy will stop going as soon as you pick them up, so don't hesitate here and then take them out to their potty spot as quickly as possible.

Now, there have been a lot of false options that have been given on what to do when your puppy goes potty inside. These things are going to reinforce a negative behavior at best and can make the puppy aggressive in the worst. Some of the things that you need to make sure that you never do when you see your puppy going potty inside include:

1. Scold the puppy for an accident that you did not personally see them do.

2. Just watch your puppy when they have this accident without doing anything to put a stop to it.

3. Yell or be really aggressive in the manner that you use to scold the puppy.

4. Put your puppy into the crate as a form of punishment for having the accident. Remember, the crate is not supposed to be a form of punishment for your puppy.

5. Rub the nose of the puppy in this accident.

Out of these myths, the first one about scolding your puppy for an accident that you didn't actually see being done is the most common mistake that dog owners will make. They may come into the room and see a pile of poop or a puddle of urine in the house, feel upset about this, and then will go on and scold the puppy for doing this. But you have to remember that when you do this, the puppy is really going to have no idea why they are in trouble. They won't even remember that they went to the bathroom in the house, and this scolding is not going to benefit either of you. Yes, it is unfortunate that they did this, but at this point, you need to just clean it up and move on, working to prevent it the next time that it happens.

Being able to debunk some of the myths about house training your puppy is so important to this guidebook. Often we think what we are doing while training the puppy is for the best, and it ends up undermining all of the good things that we try to do. Even if you have made some of these mistakes in the past, though, you can follow the tips in this chapter and in the whole guidebook to make sure that

you avoid this problem and get the best results with house training your new

puppy.

Chapter 7: Using Positive Reinforcement to Get What You Want

While this chapter is going to be brief, it is important to take a moment to explore why using positive reinforcement in all that you do with training your puppy is going to be so important. There are too many owners who are going to focus on negative reinforcement, often without realizing what they are doing, and then they wonder why the puppy is not responding to what they say or why the puppy is not doing what the owner would like.

As a new dog owner, you will find that the method for training dogs that is the most efficient and the most effective is going to be the use of positive reinforcement. Positive reinforcement is the idea of seeing the behavior that you want in a puppy and then rewarding it with praise, treats, and other rewards.

This shows the puppy that they are doing a behavior that you approve of. And since the puppy is getting this reinforcement from you and seeing that they are doing things properly, they are going to be happy to keep on with that behavior.

Let's take a look at a quick question here. What do you think would make you more determined and excited to complete a task?

1. Would you be more motivated to complete a task that you were praised for doing correctly?
2. If every time a task was assigned to you, you were automatically given a negative stimulus until you completed the task. Once the task is done, you see that the negative stimulus is gone, but there isn't any praise for the work that you did?

It is probably pretty safe to guess that most people are going to find that the first example, the one where they get the praise for completing the task at hand, is the one that they would find enjoyable and the one where they would strive to actually complete things.

The first example is going to show us what positive reinforcement is all about. But the second one is going to show us what negative reinforcement is all about. Just like you would respond to the first one, your dog is going to respond to the positive reinforcement as well.

The reason that they are going to respond to this is that the puppy knows that they are going to be given some kind of reward, whether it is a treat or some praise or something else when they complete the task. This is going to give them the motivation that they need to do the task and complete it over and over again. Plus, the positive reinforcement is going to make sure that your puppy is having a lot of fun with the training and will keep the puppy in good spirits while you do the training.

Examples of Positive Reinforcement

The best way for you to get the puppy to do what you want during training and other times is to focus on positive reinforcement. This is a bit different than what you may have seen with some of the training that your parents and others did while you were growing up. But it is more effective and can go a long way in helping you to get the puppy trained faster and more effectively. As you may have noticed, if you used any negative reinforcement on your puppy before, this kind of thing is going to reinforce some negative behavior that you probably don't want the puppy to have.

When you use positive reinforcement, you are going to focus on training the puppy in a positive way. Basically, when the puppy does something that you want, you are going to praise them, give them a reward, and make sure that they get a lot of attention. The point of this is that when you provide the positive reinforcement, the puppy wants more of it, and they are going to connect the positivity with that action, and they are going to do more of it.

Of course, this is not instant. The puppy is learning, and they are going to be a bit impulsive in the beginning. This means that you may not be able to get them to obey and listen the first few times that you use this behavior with them. But, the more you do it, the more consistent you are with it, and the more elaborate the praise, the faster the puppy will learn.

There are some different options that you can use when it comes to positive reinforcement, and the choice is going to be based on what seems to work the best for you. For example, some people find that working with lots of praise and petting will work. Some rely on treats. And others may provide some other kind of reward to your puppy.

A note on the treats, though. While these are going to be powerful motivators for your puppy, you do need to be a bit careful with them, especially if you are already working with teaching commands to your puppy. You don't want to fill the puppy up with these treats and make them miss out on their meals because they are too full. This is why using some other positive reinforcement options, for the most part, can help to keep your puppy healthy. If you do throw in a treat on occasion for really good behavior, that is fine. Maybe break up the pieces a bit so that the puppy still gets something but doesn't fill themselves up too much on the treats between meals.

Positive reinforcement is going to be a much better option to go with when you are trying to make sure that your puppy does the actions that you want. It does take some time, and you need to have a bit of patience when you are using it. But it will result in faster and more effective training methods than using any other type of reinforcement when you work with your puppy.

Examples of Negative Reinforcement

Many dog owners who run into trouble when it comes to training their puppies find that it happens when they use negative reinforcement. This happens when we use negative experiences in order to try and train their puppies. This is going to either reinforce the puppy to do the behavior that you don't want or make them more aggressive in order to fight back against the behavior.

Sometimes the negative reinforcement is going to be on purpose. If you are hitting your puppy, rubbing their nose in any accidents that they have, or even spraying them with a spray bottle of water to get them to behave, then you are using negative reinforcement, and it is likely that you know this. And if you don't realize that this is negative reinforcement, then it is time to stop and correct those behaviors right away.

Other times the behavior may not be something that you realize you are doing. For example, if you scold the puppy or get mad when they chew on the furniture and when they have an accident in the home, you are using negative reinforcement. Your first instinct may be to yell and get mad. But all this is doing is showing the puppy that they are able to get attention this way, even if it is negative attention. This gets worse if you ignore the puppy when they are doing the good behaviors that you want and only giving them attention when they are doing the bad things.

In some cases, you may find that it is going to make your puppy more aggressive when you use negative reinforcement. It is going to teach your puppy that they need to act out against you to get you to stop the yelling or the hitting or the other options.

Whether the negative reinforcement is done intentionally or not, it is still a good idea for you to learn how to make it stop and focus instead on working with positive reinforcement. This encourages the puppy to behave in the manner that you would like rather than encouraging them to act in a way that you don't really approve of for them.

Which One Is the Best?

As you should be able to see with some of the different examples that we have been talking about with reinforcement, it is easy to see why positive reinforcement is going to be the best. For some people, this may seem a bit strange, and they may not know how to change up some of the habits that they had before in order to deal with this new option. But in reality, if you want to hurry up the training process, see better results, keep the training session fun, and make sure that you don't encourage behaviors that are bad or aggressive behavior from the dog, then it is best to stick with positive reinforcement.

Remember, when you add in some positive reinforcement to the training sessions that you do, this is not only going to make it more fun for your puppy, but it will make things more fun for you during the training sessions as well. Plus, think of how great it is going to feel when your puppy is fully trained and acting just like you want them to!

Chapter 8: The Top Commands to Teach Your Puppy

This chapter is where we get to some of the fun stuff about training! We are going to look at some of the steps that you can take in order to teach your puppy some basic commands. There are a lot of different commands that you are able to teach your puppy, but we are going to focus on some of the basic ones that will make your life with your puppy a little bit easier. Some of the basic commands that we need to take a look at include:

Sit

Teaching your puppy how to sit can be a stepping stone to making sure that the puppy is a well-trained dog. When the puppy can sit on command, it helps them to learn some self-control. This method of teaching your puppy to sit is going to teach them how to sit down physically but can be a good way for the puppy to learn how to calm down mentally and engage their focus on you. Before you try moving on to any other trick or command, make sure that your puppy has mastered sitting. Some steps that you can use to help with the teaching of the sit command includes:

1. Have the puppy face you. Tell the puppy to "sit" while you hold out a treat in the hand position of your choice.
2. After saying sit once, you are not going to repeat the word again.
3. Put the treat to the nose of your puppy.

4. Move the hand so that it goes slowly forward, from the direction you are in, towards the dog as if you are going to move the treat over the head of the puppy.

    a. The reason that we do this is that it is an automatic way to get the puppy to lower their butt as they try to get to the treat.

5. Once the puppy has their butt on the floor, you can reward them using the treat and the clicker word.

6. During this process, it is important for you to go at the pace of your puppy, and you need to keep the treat on their nose. Also, never force the puppy to sit down by pushing their butt onto the floor. This isn't going to teach the puppy anything since you are forcing it, and it can cause some harm to the hips of the puppy if you are too forceful.

7. In the next fifteen to twenty minutes, repeat this exercise as many times as the puppy will do it to help reinforce the command.

As you go through this process, do not start to feel discouraged if the puppy is not sitting down the first time you do it. Some puppies don't realize what is going on and that they need to lower their butt to get the treat. But patience and persistence is the best way for you to get them to start listening to you. If the puppy starts to give up on the treat and doesn't seem like they are focused any longer, saying their name or using a kissy noise can be a good way to get their attention back on you.

Lay Down

After you and your puppy have worked on the sit command for a bit, and the puppy has got this part mastered, it is time to move on to the second command of lay down. You must make sure that the puppy knows how to sit before you start working with the lay down command because if you start teaching them too many commands at once, then you are just going to add confusion to the mix.

When the puppy is ready to learn how to lay down, get them to sit in front of you. Next, hold the treat in one hand, and then using the other hand, signal the puppy to lay down by using a hand gesture that had your pointer finger pointing down to the ground in front of the puppy's face. Some of the other steps that you need to use to work on the laying down command include:

1. Put the treat that you are using up to the nose of the puppy and then start to slowly lure the puppy down. You can do this by moving the hand down to the floor, somewhere between their paws. Go at the pace for your dog.

2. Once your hand with the treat hits the floor, slowly move it towards you and away from him along the floor. This motion should be enough to get the dog to lower themselves into a laying position.

3. Once you are able to get the puppy to lay down all of the way, make sure to say the clicker word and give them a treat.

4. Repeat this exercise as many times as you can in the next 15 minutes to help the puppy get the idea down.

Keep in mind with this one that the laying down command is going to force your puppy to focus a bit longer before they are able to get the treat that they want. There are going to be times when the puppy wants to give up before you are able to finish with the final position. Don't get frustrated with this; just keep trying, and your puppy will start to catch on to what you want them to do.

Stay

Teaching your puppy how to stay where you want, even when they want to run off and do something else, is a great training tool that you should work on once the puppy learns how to sit and lay down. It is also a command that can take some time to learn, so bring on the patience. Think of how much self-control you have to teach to a small puppy and how long they need to maintain their attention span in order to actually stay put when you want them to.

There are different methods that you can use for this one, but sometimes it is easiest to get the puppy to stay when you have them in the lay down position. This means that they are going to be less likely to want to move when they can lay all the way down rather than sitting, but you definitely can teach this command in either position.

The hand position that we need to work with for the stay command is to put your hand up, palm facing the puppy, and fingers together. Think of the hand position that you would use when trying to stop someone from coming towards you. Once you have the hand position and have used the command "stay" to the puppy, the other steps to this process that you need to follow includes:

1. With your hand out, take a step back using both feet.

2. After the two steps back, return back to the position you were at to start.

3. If your puppy was good and stayed seated that entire time, reward them with a treat and with the clicker word.

   a. Keep in mind that this is a puppy, and they probably will not want to stay still. If your puppy does get up before you can return to them, tell them "uh-uh" and get them to go back into the seated position.

   b. For the first few sessions, this may be as far as you are able to get. And that is just fine. The puppy naturally wants to follow you. Just work with them until you can get them to stay seated the whole time.

4. Once the puppy stays seated, try taking two steps back and then returning before the reward and the clicker word.

5. Keep increasing the distance that you decide to walk away from the pup, seeing how long you can go away before they start getting up again. Do this until the puppy starts to understand the command that you are giving them.

6. Repeat this exercise many times until the puppy learns how to stay put.

Wait

After you are done teaching your puppy how to stay, it is time to teach them how to wait. This is a very useful command that you can work with, but often it is underused. It can be applied to teaching your puppy to wait for their food, wait to get their leash off, wait to get out of the crate, and more. It is a great way to teach your puppy a bit of self-control and patience, which is something that all dog owners need at some point or another.

Teaching self-control to the puppy is going to be the key to having a dog that is well trained and can do a great job with all the areas of obedience. Definitely take some time to teach your puppy how to listen to this command. When you are ready to start with, it put the puppy in the position that you would like them to wait in. You may find that sitting or lying down is going to work for this. The best hand signals to use here is to have your pointer finger going up. The steps that you can use to make this happen includes:

1. Tell your puppy to wait and then use the wait hand signal.

2. While the puppy is in the seated position, preferably in the crate where feedings are supposed to happen, slowly lower the food bowl down to where they can eat.

3. If the puppy sees the bowl of food and starts to jump up or get at the food in other ways, you raise the bowl back up while saying "uh-uh."

4. Get the puppy back into the seated position and then start again. If the puppy is younger or has a lot of energy, you may have to repeat these steps a few times in order to get them to listen to you.

    a. Do not set the bowl of food all the way down until the puppy has actually patiently waited for you to lower it without them getting away from the seated position. Be aware that this can take a bit of time.

5. After you have been able to set the food bowl down, see if you are able to get the puppy to wait for another second, and then say, "OK."

    a. If you see that the puppy starts to go for the food before you say the word "OK," you can tell them "uh-uh" and pick up the bowl before trying again.

b. "OK" is going to be the release word for your puppy, and it will tell them that it is now fine to stop waiting, and they can eat the food that is in front of them.

c. As you go through this process, you will want to lengthen the amount of time that the puppy is going to wait between setting the bowl down and saying OK. This takes a bit longer but will get the puppy used to waiting until you give the orders to do something.

Come

The next command that we are going to look at is the one to come. When you do this one, you are going to teach your puppy how to come when you call them. This is also one that a lot of pet owners are going to forget to teach, and it can lead to some issues with the puppy not listening to you. This is a foundational command that you should work with your puppy on for years to come. You may use it to keep the puppy near you, when there is danger, and more.

Be prepared for this one to take a bit longer than some of the other ones. The puppy has to let you move away from them and then has to move to meet you. There are a number of steps that this will entail working with, but this is a great one to focus your attention on and make sure that you can get them to really listen to you. When you are ready to teach your puppy this command, you can follow these steps:

1. When you are working with this command, make sure that you start out in an enclosed area. This makes it easier in case your puppy decides not to listen because they are limited in the space they have to run away.
2. Take your puppy off the leash and allow them to have some time to just explore and roam around.
3. When you are ready, say the name of the puppy and then use the command "Come" in a positive voice while also holding on to a treat.
   a. Keep in mind that you want to associate this command with positivity.
   b. Your goal is to get the dog to come every time that you call them. For this to happen, the puppy needs to be conditioned to think that something positive is going to happen when they come to you.
4. If your puppy doesn't end up coming over to you right away, that is fine. You can make some kissy noises or do another thing that will get their

attention to make sure that they see the treat that you are offering. Be patient here and work on redirecting the attention of the puppy until he comes to you.

5. When the puppy does come to you, make sure that you reward them with the treat, as well as the clicker word. Do this even if it took a long time for the puppy to make their way over to you. They did listen, even if it took longer than you wanted.

6. Repeat this exercise many times until the puppy starts to come right over to you.

Leave It

The next command that we need to take a look at is "leave it." This can be a beneficial command to train your puppy, considering that they often like to be adventurous and get into everything. When you decide to use this command when the puppy is heading towards something that you don't want them to be in, you are going to see some great results. As the puppy wants to explore and see things, there are many times when this kind of command is going to be a good one to use.

Now, there are going to be a few methods that you are able to use when it comes to the command of "leave it." The first method is going to follow the steps below to make things happen.

1. Any time that the puppy starts to go for, or is already into something that you want them to leave alone, firmly tell the puppy, "leave it."

2. Remember to only tell them the command once. You can use their name or another sound to get their attention.

3. If you find that the puppy is not responding to this, put a treat or some other toy on their nose and lure them over to listening to you.

4. Once the puppy does decide to leave the object, tell them "Yes" and use the clicker word of your choice. A reward is a good way to reinforce this idea, as well.

5. Remember that your reward for this one needs to be really motivating. You are trying to get the puppy to leave something alone that they are interested in. If the reward is not good, then they are more likely to ignore you and go after the other thing.

The above method is going to work well for most puppies, and it is definitely one you can work with. But another option that you may want to try working with as well, depending on your puppy and whether or not they respond to the first method, is the second method we will tell you about below:

1. Have the puppy start this training session by lying down.
2. Put down a treat on the ground, covering it with your hand if necessary.
3. Tell your pup to "leave it."
4. Once the puppy looks at you rather than the treat, tell them "Yes" and reward them with the treat from the other hand.
5. Remember, you need to practice this one a bit. It is going to help the dog realize that if they leave the first thing, they are going to get something better, which makes them respond better to you.

Touch

Touch can be a great command to work with, and it is almost like a trick that you are able to do with your puppy. Touch is going to be a great way to teach your puppy to target something and then touch it with their nose. It is a good way to get the brain of your puppy to move and even to keep their focus when it is needed. Some of the steps that you are going to be able to use in order to teach your puppy how to respond to the touch command will include:

1. Make sure that you sit down with the puppy facing you.
2. Hold a treat or some other reward in your one hand.
3. Command your dog to "Touch" and then hold out the hand that doesn't have the treat, so it is flat in front of the nose of your dog while holding onto the treat in the other hand.

a. Once the puppy starts to get the hang of this kind of command, it will no longer be necessary to have the treat in your hand, and you can just put the hand where you would like.

4. In the beginning, you want to put the touching hand six inches or so away from the nose of your dog.

5. As soon as you are able to get the nose of your dog to touch your hand, you can reward him with the treat you have and the clicker word you choose to use.

6. You should never give your dog the treat in the hand that you want them to touch.

7. If you find that the dog is getting the hang of this trick pretty quickly, you can remove the treat and no longer use it at all.

8. As you progress with your puppy, keep moving your touching hand higher above the nose of your dog, adding in a bit of difficulty with it.

Shake

Now we are going to move a bit more into some of the different tricks that you are able to do when you work with your puppy. But the way that you do this is going to be pretty similar to the commands that we were doing before. Think of how much fun it is going to be when you want to get your puppy to shake your hand.

You will find that most puppies are going to take some time to learn how to do this trick. But if you have already spent some time teaching them some of the other commands, it may be a bit easier. As always, your job is to be patient and persistent with this and work on it each day until your puppy is ready to go with it. Some of the steps that you are able to use in order to teach your puppy how to shake with you include:

1. Make sure that you begin this with the puppy facing you.

2. Use the command "shake" and make the shake hand gesture with your hand out, palm out, and waiting.

3. Place the treat right up to one side of your pup's chest.

   a. This one is going to take a bit of patience and can be harder for the puppy to figure out what exactly you want them to do.

   b. Most pups are going to try to bite at the treat and will take some extra pains in order to get to the treat.

4. As soon as the puppy starts to paw at the treat, or even if they just start to lift the paw, immediately reward them with the treat and the clicker word.

For this kind of exercise, if you find that your pup is standing up and getting out of the seated position that you put them in, this is fine. Once they figure out that they are able to get the reward when they lift up their paw, they will figure out that it is easier for them to lift up the paw while they are seated. However, when you first start with this exercise, begin it with the puppy in the seated position before you begin.

Heel

The next command that is on our list is going to be heel. Teaching your puppy how to heel can be one of the most beneficial skills that you can teach them. If you are able to focus on this command with them when they are young, they will know how to behave when you get them older. One big behavioral problem that can happen with a puppy or dog when they get older is that they will pull on the leash while walking. Teaching your puppy how to heel is going to avoid this issue and can make walking a bit easier.

Before we get into some of the steps that we need to take in order to teach your puppy how to heel, we need to look at some tips for loose leash walking. First, remember to work with positive reinforcement. You also want to walk with a leash that is loose and never tighten it because this puts some strain on either end of the leash. You also should consider being as consistent as possible with what side your puppy needs to walk on. Pick a side and keep them there.

With these two things in mind, it is time to see how you can teach your puppy when and how to heel at the right time. The steps to making this happen will include:

1. Position the leash so it is on your arm or wrist, but make sure that it is still a bit loose.

2. If you have the puppy on the right side, make sure to hold onto the end of the leash with your left hand and grab it with the right hand down by your side. If you are holding onto the puppy on the left side, then you can flip these instructions around.

3. If you find that the puppy will stay near your side the whole time, then the second hand on the leash won't be necessary.

4. Get into a position where your puppy is on the side that you choose, and then get their attention.

5. Your goal with this one, if you can, is to get the puppy to be as calm and focused as possible so that they can pay attention to the command that you use. Have the puppy sit by you and then reward with the treat and the clicker word.

6. Say the name of your puppy, and then ask them to "heel." Keep looking at the puppy as you continue to walk.

7. Any time that the puppy looks up at you, you should say the clicker word. Depending on how often the puppy looks at you, you can provide them with a treat with the clicker word or just on occasion.

   a. The more that you see the puppy look up at you, the less you should reward with a treat so that you can slowly wean off this.

8. When it is time, take one step forward and see if you can get the attention of your puppy. Ideally, they are going to stay next to you and will heel rather than trying to pull forward.

   a. If you find that the puppy is losing their focus on you at any time, say their name or use the kissy noise, but never repeat the command more than once.

   b. If the puppy keeps the focus on you and the leash is loose, keep on walking. If the puppy tightens the leash and pulls forward, then stop with the walking.

9. Your goal here is to get the puppy to walk back over to you and get the leash loose. If the puppy doesn't do this, say their name and get their attention. If they still don't come back to you, take a step back, and see if the puppy will follow you. Last case scenario that they aren't listening to you, then lure them back with a treat.

10. Once the puppy is back to you again, use the clicker word and offer a treat. Repeat this exercise a bunch of times until the puppy is able to learn how to listen to you and do what you are asking with the heeling.

You want to make sure that with this one that you are picking out a treat that your puppy really likes. Your goal with heel is to teach the puppy how to listen to you and stop moving or pulling on the leash. This means that the reward needs to be greater than whatever else may be catching their attention at the time. Go all out with this one and pick out some of the best treats to get the puppy to listen to you.

There are some puppies who struggle with heel because they are resistant to working with the leash. If this is your puppy, then you should consider working with a harness when teaching the puppy how to heel, and even when you want to introduce them to leash walking in general. Most puppies and older dogs are going to respond to the harness so much better than using the leash for heeling and for working with the leash for walking in any form.

There are a lot of different commands that you are able to work with when it is time to teach your puppy how to listen to you. Most of these are critical commands that can get the puppy to listen to what you want them to do and to keep them out of harm, though a few of them can be almost like fun tricks that you can do together. Make sure that you take your time and go at the speed that works the best for your puppy. They will learn if you are consistent with the treats and continue doing the rewards and the clicker word each time that they succeed in doing what you would like.

Chapter 9: Dealing with Separation Anxiety

Separation anxiety is a big problem that some dogs will deal with. This is when your dog will get stressed or upset when you try to leave them anywhere. A dog that has this issue is going to cry, howl, bark, pace, destroys objects, have some accidents in the house, or want to get out of the crate. It is possible that some of these behaviors are learned, and they are going to act out badly because you, as the owner, allowed it. How are you supposed to know the difference between separation anxiety and bad behaviors?

If you have a puppy that is truly dealing with separation anxiety, you will notice that they are actually going through some emotional stress any time that you leave. If the puppy is just barking to get what they want or for attention, then this is not really separation anxiety at all. This is why it is important to know if there is separation anxiety or if it is a learned behavior because the course of action that you take with each one is going to make a big difference.

When your puppy already has true separation anxiety, then this is something that you are able to work with. It is going to take some time, but it is something that is manageable when you use the right approach to take care of the issue. You will find, though, that each case of separation anxiety is unique. There is no one concrete answer out there about what is going to cause anxiety, and it can be caused by a few different genetic and environmental factors. Some factors that can cause this anxiety will include:

1. Some of the things that may have happened to the puppy in the past before you got them.
2. How long you leave them all on their own each day.
3. Was the puppy trained in the crate properly? If you don't associate the crate with a lot of positivity, then the puppy could have some anxiety about being in it.
4. How the owner responds to some of the unwanted behaviors that the puppy tries to use.

Of course, there are also some puppies that are just going to be more attached to their owners when they are young, and this makes them more likely to develop this separation anxiety. Working through this is going to be a bit different process for each puppy depending on the circumstances and some of the behaviors that come with the dog. Before we get into that, though, we need to take a look at some of the most common mistakes that dog owners are often going to make that can encourage the separation anxiety to get worse. Some of these mistakes that you need to avoid include:

Rewarding Behaviors That You Don't Want

The most common reason why a puppy is going to develop learned behaviors that are not separation anxiety is that the owner rewarded unwanted behaviors rather than good behaviors. In fact, without even knowing what they were doing, many times, the owners would feed into the bad behaviors that their puppy was using.

Think about how you react when the puppy is whining or crying? Do you ask them what is the matter and act sympathetic for what they are doing? When they bark to get attention, are you likely to give in to the barking and give them the attention that they want? As an owner, it is likely that you are going to respond to these behaviors in a way that is bad at least a few times.

To reverse what you are doing here, you need to remember that you have to reward the good behaviors, and ignore or correct, the bad behaviors. If your puppy is dealing with bad behaviors that make them whine and bark when you leave, learning how to ignore these and work just with rewarding the good behaviors is going to make a big difference in how they respond to you.

Making the Greetings and Goodbyes Too Long

Another common method that owners are going to make the separation anxiety worse with their puppy is making greetings and goodbyes too long or too big of a deal. Think about how you act when you get home. Do you ever greet the dog in an excited way and talk to them in a higher voice? It is likely that you are excited to see your puppy after being gone all day long, but making this big of a deal out of being reunited with them is going to really make the separation anxiety that your puppy is feeling so much worse.

This means that if you want to make sure that your puppy remains calm when you come home, you need to be calm as well during both of these times. Make the greetings and farewells less important so that the puppy stays calm as well. You can say hi to them and see them, but you need to do it in a calm manner to keep them relaxed as well.

Leaving the Puppy Alone in a Bad Environment

And finally, another bad mistake that a lot of dog owners will do is to put the dog in a poor environment. It can also matter how you introduce this kind of place to your puppy. Often leaving the puppy in the crate is going to be the best, but we want to make this a place of comfort and not one that the puppy is going to feel punished in. Plus, if you leave the puppy there for eight hours or longer a day while you are at work, then you need to make sure that you let them out to play, run around outside, and explore so they aren't in the crate all of the time.

Dealing with separation anxiety is going to be really hard to work with, but there are a few different things that you are able to do in order to help prevent it. To help your puppy not gain anxiety based on the crate they are in all day, you should allow the puppy to get used to the crate when you are actually home, along with the times when you are gone. If the puppy sees the crate as a good place, as a place they can call their own and relax in, whether you are home or not, they are less likely to have anxiety when they are put inside of it.

Allow your puppy to explore the crate when you are home. This helps the puppy to see the crate as a good place, rather than them associating the crate with being left alone. This practice makes the dog realize that just because they have to go into the crate does not necessarily mean they are going to be left alone for a long time.

For example, if you start out this process by putting the puppy into the crate for shorter periods of time, such as when you run out to get the mail or just walk around the block, it is slowly going to condition the puppy so that they grow more comfortable with the time they spend in the crate. As they get accustomed to the crate and being alone for shorter periods, you can then work to increase the amount of time they are in this crate. Go from getting the mail to running some short errands and so on until you are gone for eight hours.

While you can't avoid the fact that you need to go to work and the puppy will have to stay in the crate for longer periods of time, the idea with this is that with some of the shorter periods of time added into it, the puppy is not going to feel so worked up before you leave. They are less likely to feel like you will be gone forever each time that you try to put them into the crate.

As a final reminder here, separation anxiety is going to be a long process that some owners will need to work on over the entire span of the life of the dog. This can be frustrating and discouraging if you want to go with a fix that is a bit quicker, but it is the best way to keep your cool and calm and to ensure that you keep working on it for the good of the puppy and the good of your own sanity as well.

Another thing that can sometimes cause some of this separation anxiety is if a major change happens in the life of the puppy. When these happen, they can cause some forms of separation anxiety even in a dog that never showed signs of this in the past. And sometimes, situations that may not seem like a big deal to us as humans are going to be enough to challenge the puppy and make them feel this kind of anxiety.

If you notice that your puppy is starting to show signs of being anxious when you leave, especially if they were not like this before, then it is time to take a look at what changes may be happening in their world and what you can fix. It may be a simple change that you barely noticed, but it made a big deal to the puppy. Fixing it and getting them accustomed to the change, or removing the change if it is not that important to you, can help the puppy be more comfortable and get back to their old way of doing things.

There are a lot of changes that can happen in the life of your puppy that may cause them to deal with separation anxiety in the process. There could be a change in routine, a move to a new home, or a new owner. Remember that all three of those are going to show up when you try to bring your puppy home for the first time. Being patient and thinking about the needs of your puppy and learning how to work through the separation anxiety is going to make life easier for both of you.

Separation anxiety is going to show up at different times for each puppy, and it is going to depend on the puppy that you have, their personality, and some of the life experiences that they may have had in the past. You may find that the anxiety can start as early as when you walk through the door with a new puppy, or a big life change could be the root cause that you have to deal with. Understanding this and looking for some of the signs of separation anxiety will make a difference.

You are able to prevent some of the separation anxiety that your puppy is feeling just by avoiding some of the mistakes that we have talked about in this chapter. The thing to remember here, even if you are following the advice that is above, is that there are some puppies that will come to your home with a very attached personality, and they may need to go through some extra socialization and steps in order to prevent the anxiety from starting in the first place.

If you find that your puppy is like this, and some of the symptoms that come with separation anxiety start to show up, you may find that having your puppy go to dog daycare or having someone come over during the day to play with and walk to your puppy can help. This helps the puppy to get a lot of socialization and can be the best way to help them realize that you are not the only person in the world. Often just a bit of time with this is enough to help the puppy get over their issues with separation anxiety.

This doesn't have to be an all the time thing. Even just one day of dog daycare for your puppy is enough to give them the socialization that they need and can get them out of the house rather than being alone. Doing this once a week for a few months can help the puppy see that they are not alone, even when you leave, and will make it easier for your puppy to get out some of that pent up energy from being home waiting for you all day too.

Separation anxiety is an issue that some dog owners are going to need to deal with when they bring a new puppy home. Some dogs will not have this issue, and others are going to find that it is something major that they need to deal with. Before you jump in and try to make things better for the puppy, make sure that you are dealing with true separation anxiety and not just some bad behaviors where the puppy is trying to get what they want or to get your attention.

Once you have determined that your puppy is actually dealing with separation anxiety, you can take the steps that are needed to help put a stop to it. Understanding the changes that are going on with your puppy, learning how to be calmer when you leave and come home, and teaching the puppy about the crate in a more positive manner, so they don't feel worried when you leave them in there, are all important. When all of this comes together, you will find that it is much easier for you to get your puppy to feel comfortable and safe, and to stop

some of the separation anxiety when you leave, even when they have to be home

alone for some time.

Chapter 10: Tough Dog Problems and How to Deal with Them

Once you are able to train your dog a few of the commands from the last chapter, you will find that the puppy is going to behave the way that you would like. They will listen to the commands that you give and will get along with the family. However, each puppy is going to have a different kind of personality, and it is possible that they will still deal with some problems that you will need to take care of.

Some puppies are not going to have any of these tough dog problems, and some are going to have a few that you need to deal with. Learning what your puppy is going to do when others come around and what behaviors you need to fix and fixing them as quickly as possible can be the key to having a puppy behave the way that you want. Some of the most common tough dog problems that your puppy may show and the steps you can take to deal with them include:

Jumping up on Other People

Do you find that your puppy likes to jump up on you and other people? For those who know what this is like, know that this is actually a behavior issue that should not be encouraged. Owners find that it can be hard to get dogs, no matter the age, to stop jumping up on them and some of the other people who are around them. Even if you don't feel like this is a big deal right now, think about how you are going to feel about the dog jumping on you or someone else when they are 100+ pounds? It is better to train your puppy to not jump on anyone from a young age. It is easier this way and ensures that they aren't going to be toppling other people over either.

First, we need to take a look at why the puppy is likely to jump on you or other people. For the most part, this is because they are excited. They see you or someone else comes through the door, and because they don't have the necessary self-control yet, and they want to jump up to show how excited they are to see you. Or, there may be times when the puppy is going to jump up because they see some item in your hand that they want, and they jump up to try and get it.

Either way, it is important to learn how to stop the puppy from jumping up on you and knocking you and others down. You need to remember to be consistent. You can't discourage the jumping one day and then be excited to see them another day and be fine with the jumping. Also, you can't have your cake and eat it too. You can't allow the dog to jump on you and then train them not to jump on other people. This confuses the puppy and won't help you or them out at all. You have to decide that jumping is bad behavior and then work to train them not to do it.

The good news here is that you are able to follow a simple process in order to get your puppy to listen to you and do what you would like. As with all of the unwanted behaviors that we are going to bring up in this chapter, you need to be strict about not allowing the puppy to jump on you ever. As you are going through the training process, and you see that the puppy is trying to jump on you, use the following steps to help prevent the behavior:

1. Tell the puppy, "OFF."

2. Turn your body around so that your puppy is looking directly at your back.

3. When you move the body so that it is turned around, the puppy is going to automatically get their paws back down on the floor and where they should be.

4. After the puppy has put their paws down, you can turn to face the puppy and then redirect them until they are sitting down.

5. Once the puppy listens and actually sits down, pet them, and reward them, showing the puppy that this is the way you want them to get your attention.

6. Now, there are going to be some times when the puppy will attempt to jump up on you again. If they start to do this, stop providing them with attention, and go through the steps above again. Only give the puppy some attention and affection when they are sitting down.

7. Practice with this each time that you come into the house, and even purposely leave for a few minutes so that you get some more practice. Over time, this is going to become a habit, and the puppy will learn that they are not supposed to jump on you.

The point of doing this is to show the puppy that they are only going to get attention when they sit, rather than getting any attention when they are up and moving and jumping on others. This will help stop them from jumping on you and can do some wonders for teaching them some self-control along the way.

Destructive Chewing

Another issue that a lot of puppies will fall into is that they will start to chew on a lot of things that they shouldn't, many items that you do not allow and are not part of their chew toys. When you first bring a puppy home, especially if they are only about eight weeks old, remember that they don't know what is and what is not allowed to chew on. You have to step up and teach them these rules. Sure it is easy to get frustrated with the puppy when they chew on the wrong thing, but you have to be proactive and teach your puppy what is appropriate behavior, especially when it comes to chewing.

While it may feel like the puppy is purposely being naughty and just had to go after your favorite pair of shoes, remember that there are a lot of reasons why the puppy is chewing in the first place. They aren't trying to be naughty, and they aren't trying to make life more difficult for you. Some of the reasons that your puppy may be chewing on things include:

1. Dogs have a need that is instinctual that tells them to chew on things.
2. Chewing is a good outlet for most puppies when it is time to exert energy. Your dog could be chewing on a variety of items when they have a lot of energy that they need to get rid of or when they feel a bit bored with their activities.
3. Similar to what we see with infants, puppies like to put objects into their mouths in the hopes of figuring out what the object is and what they should do with it.
4. Puppies will often chew when they are teething. This chewing method is going to be a good way for them to soothe their gums.

Your dog is going to chew, and they need to chew, no matter if they are a brand new puppy or you have had them around for some time. You can't stop them from chewing, but you can control what they are allowed to do this with. You just need to pick out the right chew toys or items that you are going to give to the puppy and teach them what they can chew on and what they need to avoid.

The good news is there are a few things that you are able to do in order to make sure the puppy is going to chew on the right items and that they won't start to chew on some of your favorite items or on anything that they shouldn't have their mouths on. Some of the rules that you are able to follow when it comes to this include:

1. Always have some approved chewing objects that you can give to your puppy. Your puppy is going to chew no matter what, so make sure that you provide them with some toys or objects that they are allowed to chew on instead of getting mad when they chew on items that you don't approve of.

2. Be strict with what they can chew on and what they can't chew on. In the beginning, you have to be strict on this and may have to keep the puppy confined to one area. But this is their learning period, and you are going to see the best results when you can keep track of the puppy and make sure that they don't get ahold of things they shouldn't have.

3. Redirect the puppy to an object that you approve of for them to chew on. The puppy is sometimes going to get away from you and will try to chew on something that they should not. When you catch them in the act, don't try to shout or yell or get mad about it. This just encourages them because the puppy sees that they are getting attention from this. Instead, when you

find them, say "NO" and then redirect them over to an item that is designed for them to chew on.

Pulling on the Leash

Another common issue that you will see when you bring home a new puppy is that they like to pull on the leash. This one seems to be a really hard problem for most dog owners to deal with, and it seems like most owners are going to allow their puppy to pull on the leash forever. The good news is that it is possible to train your puppy to stop pulling on the leash, making things a whole lot easier for you.

The bottom line to remember here is that your leash should never be tight when you try to take the puppy on a walk. A loose leash is going to be the standard that you set, and it means that there is a little bit of slack on the leash between the puppy and you. There are a few reasons why you would want this to happen. It is going to teach the puppy that you are the pack leader, and they should respect you. You don't want the puppy to start to think that they get to lead you all the time. When the puppy decides to make the leash tight and pulls on it, it is going to add a ton of stress and pressure to the neck, and this can be harmful to them. Pulling can also cause some damage to your own joints on the shoulders and arms. And when the puppy goes with a loose leash, it is going to become a much more enjoyable walk for both of you.

Now, this brings up the question of what you are supposed to do when the puppy decides to pull on the leash when you are walking. This may slow down your walk a bit, but you will find that most puppies are going to catch on quickly, and doing this can really make a difference in how well the walk goes. Taking some time now will help you have much more pleasant walks overall. Some of the steps that you are able to do to help stop the puppy from pulling on the leash will include:

1. Any time that you feel the dog is getting excited and starts pulling on the leash, stop right where you are and don't go any further.
2. When the puppy starts to see that you have stopped and looks back at you, work with the clicker word.
3. Wait for the puppy to walk back to you, and when the puppy does this, reward them with a treat.

4. If you notice that the puppy is not coming back to you, lure them back using the heeling position and with a treat if you need it.

5. Now, there are some times when the puppy is still not going to come over to you. If this is the case, you can take another step back. Continue to do this until the puppy starts to walk back to you.

6. Repeat this process as many times as you need during the walk until the puppy learns that the leash needs to be loose.

As you can imagine, this is going to slow down the walk for a bit. You may only want to go on a walk down the block or so until the puppy starts to get the hang of what you are doing. The good news here is that the puppy will learn, and you will get the puppy to walk alongside you, with a nice loose leash rather than one that is tight and harming both you and the puppy, in no time.

The Puppy Doesn't Want to Walk on the Leash

There are some puppies who are so excited to go on a walk that they will bounce around, and then, once you are outside, they are going to pull on the leash, and you need to work on that problem. But then there are the puppies that don't like to walk on the leash at all. This is common for puppies who haven't been exposed to the leash at all. Most of the time, they are going to catch on pretty quickly though, you just need to do a few steps in order to make this work for you. Some of the steps that you can use to get your puppy more used to the leash and doing what you want with it include:

1. Pull on the leash a bit, gently to the side while telling the command of "come" to the puppy.

2. If you find that this is not working, then call the puppy to you with a treat or something else that can be a reward.

3. If neither of the two steps above are working, you can try it with a harness and just repeat the steps that we have from above.

   a. You will find that the harness can be a nice addition because it gives you a bit more control over the puppy while making it so that you don't put too much pressure on the neck of your puppy.

4. Once the puppy listens to you and walks over, reward the puppy with a treat and a clicker word.

5. If you find that the puppy is responding pretty well with this, try calling the puppy to you without the treat, and use the clicker word on its own as a reward.

6. Repeat the process again until your puppy gets more familiar with the leash and doesn't seem to mind it as much.

Too Much Roughhousing with the Puppy

You will find that in some instances, your puppy is going to get into a really crazy mood where they will zoom around so much that they end up losing their self-control and won't behave well. When a puppy is in this kind of state, you will find that redirecting the puppy is not going to be enough. The more excitement that the puppy has, the harder it is to get the puppy to control themselves. This means that you need to step up and gain control before the puppy has its energy escalate too high.

This is going to require the whole family to get on board and making sure they are all on the same page. If the kids are working to rile the puppy up, it could get out of control before you even have a chance to slow it down a bit. The sooner you are able to slow the puppy down, the easier things are going to be for you.

What this means is if you see that the excitement of the puppy is starting to build, it is time to gain control right away. You can have them sit or do one of the other commands that get them to stop and listen to you. Sitting is a good way to force the puppy to have some self-control and calm down.

Now, there may be some times when the puppy is going to be in this state already. This means that the puppy is going to have already lost their self-control, and you and the rest of the family may need to remove yourselves from the situation so that they don't exert this loss of control onto the kids or you at this time. Another option that can work with this is to put the dog on the leash and take them outside to wear out some of that energy or let them run in the backyard. This helps to get some of that pent up energy out, and then the puppy will be able to exert self-control again.

Fearfulness

There are some puppies who are going to be more reserved and may have some fears of the world, or at least a fear of things that are unfamiliar. It is natural to want to shelter them from the things that they fear, but this actually is going to cause the puppy more harm than good. The key in cases of fearfulness is to try and expose the puppy to the things that they are afraid of, but you should do it in a positive, as well as in a gradual, manner.

If you notice that you have a puppy that seems to be afraid of trying out anything new, or they have some fears that they can't seem to get over, there are a few steps that you can try out, including:

1. Give your puppy some exposure to the thing that they are afraid of. Do this in a very slow manner so that they have time to look it over and explore it.

2. Start out with a big distance between the object the puppy is scared of and the puppy itself.

3. Associate the object of the puppy's fear with a lot of positivity. A good way to do this is to incorporate something that the puppy really likes to the situation.

4. If your puppy is motivated by food, make sure that they are given a lot of treats while you expose them to that object.

5. Slowly start to move the puppy a bit closer to the object that they are scared about. Let them have some time to gain comfort with each distance to the object.

   a. Keep in mind that slowly is going to vary based on the puppy and how they are reacting to this process. You have to go at the speed and the distance that works the best for your puppy.

   b. If you find that the puppy seems pretty comfortable and unstressed, you may be able to approach the object of their fear on that same day. But for some puppies, moving them just a bit closer each day is going to be the best option.

You will need to repeat this process again and again, going a bit closer each day, until the puppy has been able to overcome their fears. Throughout the whole process, make sure to pay attention to the body language of the puppy and learn their signals. You do not want to have them become too stressed out, and you don't want to push the puppy past their limits because this is just going to make things worse, and the puppy will start to fear the object more than before.

The Escape Artist

Hopefully, you are able to read this part of the guidebook before the puppy has been able to escape out of your home and run away. Obviously, having the puppy escape and get lost is a traumatic experience for the whole family. But if the puppy is able to do this once, then it is likely they will continue to do this again and again.

There are several reasons why the puppy is going to try and get out of the home. They are allowed to roam freely, get into things, and do anything that they want. When they are out of the home and away from you, they don't have to follow any of the rules any longer! Escaping is going to be a kind of self-rewarding behavior for a dog, and because of this fact, it is going to be a hard one to break if the puppy has already been able to do this.

This means that your goal needs to be to prevent the puppy from getting out and escaping from the home in the first place. Some of the steps that you can take to help prevent your dog from bolting or escaping from your home will include:

1. Make sure that you are fully aware of where your dog is each time that you are about to go out the door. Make sure that all of the people in the home, even visitors, are aware of this kind of rule.
2. Train your dog to sit and consistently wait before going outside can be useful for this, as well. It may take a bit more time and patience, and it is likely that the dog won't want to do it, but it helps them to know they have to sit still if they want to go out.
3. If your back yard has a fence, then you need to make sure that it is secure in every place. You do not want to have any places on the fence or in the yard where your puppy will be able to get through.
4. If you do not have a fenced in backyard, then you need to make sure that the puppy is always on a leash.

The last point that is up above is going to be important. You may be tempted to keep the puppy off the leash because they have been behaving and have not been getting off the leash lately. But this gives the puppy a perfect chance to escape.

You have to be consistent with this so that the puppy will know their boundaries.

Too Much Whining and Barking

You will find that an excessive amount of barking is going to be a really frustrating behavioral issue that you, as a new owner of a puppy, will have to deal with. This is also one of the biggest stressors that come up with a dog and its owner. This is why it is so important to solve the problem before it gets to a level that is too hard to control.

First, you need to be able to understand why the puppy is barking so much in the first place. Some of the reasons why your puppy may be barking so much to start with will include:

1. To try and get your attention
2. Because they are uncertain or fearful about something.
3. They want to be able to assert their own dominance over a passerby or another animal.

There are different steps that you will need to take based on what the puppy is barking at. If you find that the puppy is barking at you at this time, then it is because they want to gain more control, or they want your attention. Whether your puppy wants to be with the rest of the pack or they need some more exercise or something else, this is a behavior that you need to correct right away. The steps that you can take to make this work include:

1. If you notice that the puppy continues to bark, turn your back to them and continue to ignore them until they stop.
2. Have some patience here because the puppy is going to continue their barking, in some cases, for a long period of time.
3. Once the puppy does stop barking, no matter how long it took, you can turn around and give the puppy lots of praise, treats, and attention.

4. Any time that the puppy starts to bark at you, repeat this process until they stop barking. This lets them know that you will only give them attention if they are not barking.

5. If you can't get the puppy to stop barking, then it is time to take a break in the crate until they are all done.

In some cases, the puppy is going to bark at passersby and animals. This issue is sometimes embarrassing when you bring your puppy in public, but some people may feel a bit frightened if they don't know your dog. Many times the owner is going to reinforce this behavior by screaming at the puppy to stop. You need to shift up the way that you respond to the barking first to get them to listen.

Let's say that the puppy is barking when they look at people or dogs through the window. Some of the steps that you are able to use in order to get the puppy to stop barking in this manner include:

1. Call the puppy's name in a positive manner so that they put their focus on you instead of the object of their attention outside.

2. The positive aspect of this is going to be the most important thing that you can do, but it is often the hardest as well. You need to find a way to be more motivating to the puppy than what they see outside.

3. Once the puppy does look over at you, reward them before refocusing their attention on something else that they like, such as a bone or a toy, so they don't get distracted again and start barking.

It is also possible that your puppy is going to start barking at some people and other animals when they are in public. You are not going to be able to demand that they listen to you in the same manner that you could when at home. But this also doesn't mean that you have to just let the puppy bark all day long while you are out in public or that you have to go home. When you have a puppy who is barking at people and other animals when they are out in public, some of the steps that you can take include:

1. If you have a puppy who is already barking, it is time to move far enough away from the focus of their bark so that they stop the barking. If you are aware of a stimulus that may cause the puppy to bark, try to start out far enough away so that they aren't going to bark at it to start with.

2. When the puppy is looking in the direction of the stimuli, call their name and do what it takes to redirect their focus back on you. When the puppy looks at you, give them a treat. This is going to help them to associate that stimulus with positivity.

3. As you get the puppy to self-control and calm down, see if you are able to move a bit closer to the stimuli. With each step, stop and redirect the puppy back to you, and get them to gain the self-control that you want.

    a. The degree you move is going to vary between each animal, so take your time and see what works for your dog.

4. During this process, make sure that you are the one who is maintaining the control, not the dog. Check on a regular basis that the puppy remains relaxed during this process.

5. If you move closer and your puppy starts to bark again, it is time to move further away and then work to focus their attention back onto you before trying again.

Being on the Furniture

If you do not want the puppy to get up on your furniture, then this is another problem that you will need to work on as soon as possible. Remember that this one is up to you. Some people don't mind the puppy being on the furniture, and some don't want the puppy there at all. Either one is fine as long as you are consistent all the way.

For those who don't want their puppy on the furniture for one reason or another, this is just fine, but you need to start early, be firm with your decision, and be consistent. It isn't going to work if you sometimes allow the puppy on the furniture, and then other times, they are not allowed up there. It also will not work if you tell the puppy not to get on the furniture, but then others in the family allow the puppy to get up there.

If you have decided that you do not want to have your puppy to be up on the furniture, some of the steps that you are going to take in order to make sure that the puppy will stay off your furniture include:

1. Be strict right from the start and make sure that the puppy is never allowed on the furniture.
2. Any time that the puppy tries to jump up on the furniture tell them "OFF."
3. Motivate the puppy to get off of your furniture and back to the floor by drawing them down with a treat or a toy.
   a. If you find that the puppy is not really willing to get off the furniture with this, then it is fine to guide the puppy down with the use of their collar to follow your No.
4. Make sure to reward the puppy with praise, a treat, and the clicker word when they do get off the furniture. Remember, with this one, that prevention is going to be the best way to work through the behavior, and if

you find that the puppy is heading for the couch, be ahead of the game and automatically direct them to sit and give them a reward in the process.

Digging

While this is not really a behavior that is going to be bad for the puppy, it can be harmful to your yard, and this may be the reason that you stop it. Of course, most people don't want to look out in their yard and see a bunch of holes everywhere, so dealing with this problem right from the start can really help.

The first thing that we need to look at here is some of the reasons that a dog is going to dig. Each dog will be a bit different, but generally, a dog is going to dig because their breed has a genetic disposition to digging, they are using this to help them get their energy out, or they feel bored.

This is one of those times when it is best to be preventative to make sure the puppy does not dig. Exercising and stimulating your puppy can help them to not get bored, and it gets all of that extra energy out so that they are not likely to dig in your yard any longer. A puppy who is exerting all of their energy by playing with their toys, chewing on bones, and getting out on walks is going to find that they have no need to go to the yard and dig some holes. If genetics are the problem, then there probably isn't much that you can do to prevent this issue. You just need to learn how to correct the behavior to get it to stop with your puppy.

If you do happen to catch the dog digging in your yard and you want to get them to stop, there are a few steps that you are able to take. Some of these steps include:

1. If you find that your dog is already digging in your yard, tell them "NO" in a firm manner and get them away and distracted from the hole.
   a. If you can, immediately redirect him to an appropriate item he can exert his energy into, such as running around the yard or chewing on a bone.
2. If you find a new hole that you didn't catch your puppy digging, there is nothing that you should do about the behavior. You need to make sure that you catch them in the act. If it is after the fact, then you are out of luck.

a. Remember that you are not able to discipline the puppy for something they did that you weren't able to catch them doing.

b. Your puppy is not going to remember that they dug the hole, even if it was just a minute ago. Scolding the puppy later on is not going to do you any good because the puppy won't have any idea what you are scolding them for.

As you can see, there are a lot of behaviors that your puppy may show off that are going to make life a bit harder when you are working with your puppy. It is best if you are able to be proactive with this process and learn how to deal with the behaviors before they get even worse. The sooner that you are able to deal with these problems, the easier it is going to be. Following the steps that are in this chapter will make it easier for you to really get your puppy to behave in the manner that you would like.

Conclusion

Thank you for making it through to the end of *Puppy Training*. Let's hope it was informative and able to provide you with all of the tools you need to achieve your goals, whatever they may be.

The next step is to spend some time working with your puppy on some of the training techniques that we brought up in this guidebook. Each puppy is going to learn how to behave in their own way, and some puppies are going to take a bit longer to behave and act the way that you want them to. But this guidebook is going to provide you with the results that you want, and before you know it, your new puppy will be able to respond to the commands that you give and will be fully trained in no time.

This guidebook was meant to be the ultimate guide to helping you really train your puppy and see some amazing results. We looked at the basics of training any command to your puppy, along with some of the specific commands that you are able to train your puppy to respond to. We looked at the importance of a crate for your puppy and how to crate train them. And we even looked at house training them so that they can be accident-free and not messing up your home. When all of this comes together, along with some of the other topics that we look at, your puppy will be trained and ready to go!

When you are trying to prepare for bringing home a new puppy, and you want to know the best steps to help them behave and follow the commands and rules that you set up in your home, make sure to check out this guidebook to help you get started.

Finally, if you found this book useful in any way, a review is always appreciated!